Latin America's
Political Economy
of the Possible

Latin America's Political Economy of the Possible

Beyond Good Revolutionaries and Free-Marketeers

Javier Santiso

translated by
Cristina Sanmartín
and Elizabeth Murry

The MIT Press
Cambridge, Massachusetts
London, England

First MIT Press paperback edition, 2007
© 2006 Massachusetts Institute of Technology

For information on quantity discounts, please email special_sales @mitpress.mit.edu.

Set in Palatino by The MIT Press. Printed and bound in the United States of America.

Library of Congress Cataloging-in-Publication Data
Santiso, Javier.
Latin America's political economy of the possible / Javier Santiso; translated by Cristina Sanmartín and Elizabeth Murry.
  p. cm.
Includes bibliographical references and index.
ISBN-10: 0-262-19542-9 (hc : alk. paper)—0-262-69359-3 (pb : alk. paper)
ISBN-13: 978-0-262-19542-3 (hc : alk. paper)—978-0-262-69359-2 (pb : alk. paper)
1. Latin America—Economic policy.   2. Latin America—Politics and government—1980– I. Title.

HC125.S2755 2006
330.98—dc22   2005058437
10 9 8 7 6 5 4 3

for Albert Hirschman

We are left empty-handed. Then the door of perception opens slightly and the other time *appears, the real time we had been seeking without knowing it: the present, the presence.*

—Octavio Paz

Contents

Foreword

In 2001 George Bush started out his first presidential term by stating that his best *amigos* were in Latin America, and that the United States' most important relationship abroad was with Mexico. This may have been an overstatement, but the underlying feeling was probably genuine. Washington could surely rejoice in Latin America's turn toward democracy: all its countries except for Cuba were governed by elected civilians. And most of these governments were busy putting into place the pro-market economic reforms the United States had long advocated.

But then came 9/11, and the alleged *amigos* were quickly forgotten. A long period of neglect, not always benign, followed. Peter Hakim, one of Washington's most seasoned Latin-watchers, wrote in the December 2005 issue of *Foreign Affairs*: "Relations between the United States and Latin America today are at their lowest point since the end of the Cold War."

Reporting on Latin America in the US media, never too abundant, has become rarer still. And when US-based

reporters do venture south of the border, they continue to
see Latin politics as the struggle between impoverished
masses and conservative elites, between good revolutionaries and free-market fundamentalists. These old
clichés, as Javier Santiso points out in this insightful
book, are grossly out of date. While the United States and
much of the world looked the other way, Latin America
has continued to change, and very fast.

The main point of the book is simple: a new kind of
political leadership has emerged in Latin America.
Unlike the left-wing ideologues of the 1960s and 1970s
and the right-wing ideologues of the 1980s and 1990s,
these new leaders are pragmatists. They are committed,
in Albert Hirschman's lovely phrase, to the "political
economy of the possible."

Chile's leaders of the last 15 years are the poster children of this new kind of leadership. An alliance of
Socialists, Social Democrats, and Christian Democrats,
they have run budget surpluses year after year, privatized infrastructure, relentlessly cut tariffs, and signed
free-trade agreements with the United States, the
European Union, Canada, China, South Korea, and a
dozen other nations. At the same time, the three Chilean
governments since 1990 have increased spending on education, health, and housing, raised taxes, strengthened
anti-trust legislation, and opposed the US war in Iraq.

The new Chilean leadership is highly trained. All the
finance ministers have doctorates from places like Yale
and Harvard. The current president, Ricardo Lagos, a

lawyer by training, has a Ph.D. in economics from Duke. But rather than adhere single-mindedly to one recipe, they tend to pick and choose among alternative approaches, and stick finally to what works.

Chile is certainly not alone in this. Brazil was led for two consecutive four-year terms by Fernando Henrique Cardoso, a world-famous sociologist who as finance minister had conquered decades of Brazilian inflation. Cardoso, much like his friend Lagos in Chile, surrounded himself with US-educated technocrats and combined orthodox fiscal and monetary policies with bold social initiatives, particularly in education. Cardoso was succeeded in office by Luiz Inácio "Lula" da Silva, a former metalworker who ran from the hard left but has governed since 2002 from the moderate center.

Ernesto Zedillo and Vicente Fox in Mexico, Valentín Paniagua and Alejandro Toledo in Peru, Andrés Pastrana and Álvaro Uribe in Colombia, Jorge Batlle and Tabaré Vásquez in Uruguay—some of these recent Latin American presidents have called themselves conservatives, others leftists; some have been quite popular and successful, others much less so. But they have two things in common: they were all constitutionally elected, and on economic issues they have been pragmatists.

One might have thought these moderate leaders would be natural partners for the United States. But with the notable exception of Uribe, they have mostly received a cold shoulder from Washington.

While the new generation of Latin presidents has had many successes, it also has failures of its own to account for. The biggest one has to do with economic growth. So much pragmatism has helped to lower inflation, to cut budget deficits, to stabilize wobbly banks, and (in some cases) to avoid currency crises. But it has not made Latin America much more prosperous. Over the last 20 years, Chile was the only country to reduce its income gap with the United States. All others have diverged, becoming relatively poorer.

Unlike much of Asia, the region is not on a path of sustained growth. In 2004, its best year in two decades, Latin America's economy expanded by 5.5 percent. In contrast, India has been averaging 6 percent growth annually for 15 years, and China's economy has grown by 10 percent for 25 years.

This poor growth and jobs performance is one reason why populism is once again rearing its ugly head in the region. Not every leader is a Lagos or a Lula. There is also Commander Hugo Chávez of Venezuela, a twice-failed putsch leader who then went on to be elected president. Under his watch, national income contracted by nearly 17 percent in 2002–03, and investment fell to a paltry 15 percent of GDP. Chávez now offers to export his Bolivarian Revolution to other countries in the region. Fidel Castro has offered his help in this task. Collaboration may also be forthcoming from Evo Morales, the newly elected president of Bolivia, who during the campaign promised to nationalize the oil and gas industries currently owned by multinational firms. And there is Argentina's Néstor Kirchner, who has tried to fight inflation by threatening to boycott supermarkets.

Javier Santiso labels Chávez, Kirchner, and Morales "neo-populists." They revel in anti-market and anti-globalization rhetoric, and promise quick fixes ranging from poverty to inequality. In a region where such promises have long been common currency, this is not surprising. What is more novel, as Santiso points out, is that even Chávez and Kirchner have shown themselves to be pragmatists of a sort, avoiding the large budget deficits and runaway inflation that routinely brought the downfall of their populist predecessors.

Showing a deep "bias for hope" (the phrase again is Hirschman's), Santiso celebrates the "profound and subtle transformation that is taking place in Latin America, stemming from the surge of economic pragmatism." But, as he acknowledges in the final chapter, "the emergence of possibilism . . . remains incomplete and fragile; it is an unfinished journey."

Whether the journey will indeed be completed is up to Latin Americans. But Washington can help along the way. By picking fights with Chávez or Morales, or trying to isolate them as it has with Castro, American policy makers would surely make these neo-populists even more popular at home. Pragmatism in American policy toward the region: that would be a historic shift indeed.

Andrés Velasco
December 2005

Acknowledgments

This book owes much to innumerable conversations, exchanges, and discussions conducted over many years. It is impossible to mention here all those who stimulated the thoughts formulated and shared here. A big thanks to everyone for their shared passion for and interest in the Americas.

A big thank you to Suzanne Santiso, Albert Hirschman, Guy Hermet, Christophe Jaffrelot, and Koldo Echebarría, without whom the book would not have seen the light of day.

An equally big thank you—the order is purely alphabetical—to my former colleagues and friends at BBVA's Economic Research Department, in particular Manolo Balmaseda, Jorge Blázquez, Octavio de Barros, Juan Carlos Berganza, Miguel Cardoso, Luis Carranza, Nathaniel Karp, Guillermo Larraín, Juan Martínez, Diane McCollum, Angel Melguizo, Rodolfo Méndez, Alejandro Neut, Giovanni di Placido, Juan Antonio and Javier Rodríguez, Miguel Sebastián, Luciana Taft, David

Taguas, David Tuesta, David Martínez Turégano, and
Joaquín Vial. I also wish to thank all the students, profes-
sors and research fellows at the Paul H. Nitze School of
Advanced International Studies (SAIS) at Johns Hopkins
University and at the Centre for International Studies
and Research at Sciences-Po Paris with whom I was able
to develop the ideas set forth here, confront these
thoughts and have continuous and always stimulating
exchanges.

Finally, a great thank you, for all the exchanged con-
versations or shared documents over the course of these
last years, to Enrique Alberola, Manuel Alcántara, Edmar
Bacha, Jessica B. Baker, Fernando Bergasa, Leslie Bethell,
Mario Bléjer, Olivier de Boysson, Ignacio Briones, Victor
Bulmer-Thomas, Guillermo Calvo, Mauricio Cárdenas,
Guillermo Cardoza, Fernando Carrillo, Roberto Chang,
Christophe Cordonnier, Guillermo de la Dehesa, Jacques
de Larosière, Henry Dougier, Carlos Elizondo, Antoni
Estevadeordal, José Antonio Fernández Rivero,
Alejandro Foxley, Ricardo Ffrench-Davis, Albert Fishlow,
Marc Flandreau, Jeffry Frieden, Alicia García Herrero,
José Gijón, José Ignacio Goirigolzarri, Ilan Goldfajn,
Mauro Guillén, Angel Gurría, Carol Graham, Martín
Grandes, Enzo Grilli, Fernando Gutiérrez, Leo Harari,
Enrique Iglesias, Paul Isbell, Alejandro Izquierdo,
Edmundo Jarquín, Jacint Jordana, Alfredo Joignant, Terry
Karl, Marta Lagos, Richard Lapper, Bénédicte Larre,
Norbert Lechner, Eduardo Lévy-Yeyati, Juan Linz,
Eduardo Lora, José Luis Machinea, Antonio Merino,

Alejandro Micco, Juan Antonio Mielgo, Francisco Monaldi, Nanno Mulder, Elizabeth Murry, Vitalino Nafría, Sebastián Nieto, Joaquim Oliveira, Mancur Olson, Alvaro Ortiz, Luisa Palacios, Ugo Panizza, Gerardo della Paolera, Ludolfo Paramio, Guillermo Perry, Adam Przeworski, Carlos Quenan, Ricardo Raphael, Riordan Roett, Alain Róuquié, Cristina Sanmartín, Carlos Santiso, Philippe Schmitter, Luis Servén, Jérôme Sgard, Dorothy Sobol, Lourdes Sola, Marcelo Soto, Ernesto Stein, Ernesto Talvi, Alan Taylor, Mariano Tommasi, Michael Tomz, Aaron Tornell, Arturo and Samuel Valenzuela, Andrés Velasco, Peter West, Laurence Whitehead, Juan Yermo, and Daniel Zovatto.

**Latin America's
Political Economy
of the Possible**

Introduction: The Waltzing Paradigms

One of the first iconographic representations of the New World can be found in Spain's great Museo del Prado. It is a tree painted 500 years ago by Hieronymus Bosch. This tree, which for the painter evoked the lands discovered by Columbus, appears in Bosch's famous triptych *The Garden of Earthly Delights* in the panel representing Paradise. From the time of their discovery, the Americas were identified by Europeans with Paradise on Earth. Therefore, in the Western imagination the new continent was depicted as a utopia where everything was marvelously possible.

The search for utopia is a constant theme in the history of the Americas. The results of this search, however, have never measured up to expectations. The golden age evolved into the age of steel, and its eternal spring turned into a long season in hell. We can summarize the failure to find utopia in the Latin American landscape by reviewing the continent's urban history, a frustrated tale of the discovery of promised lands and resplendent cities. For example, the Brazilian cities of Belo Horizonte and Porto Alegre, whose names are full of promise and optimism, have turned into immense tentacular orbs that affirm how impossible utopias are to realize—deviant paradises transformed into hells, such as Acapulco, which Carlos Fuentes rechristened "Kafkapulco." One can find many other examples of impossible utopias and monstrous deviations in the search for a better world that quickly changed the course of the search for paradise into a temporal endeavor rather than a spatial one. The continent's history developed as a series of frustrated, aborted, failed, or continually renewed attempts to reach a better tomorrow.

The search for utopia has also pervaded the history of Latin America's political economy. Since its independence, one of Latin America's core dependencies has been its belief in miracles: the miracle forged by the Marxist or free-market magicians, revolutionaries and counterrevolutionaries, on the basis of a few grand theories and paradigms. In the twentieth century—led by the Marx Brothers and the Chicago Boys, all of whom proclaimed great principles and offered to sacrifice the social realities of their countries to their monetary gods—the entire region was captivated by magical realism, blindly supporting ready-made solutions—sometimes in a violent form—which were unleashed on society and projected onto reality itself and which after a short time were exchanged for more alluring alternatives. From structuralism to monetarism, and from Marxism to free-

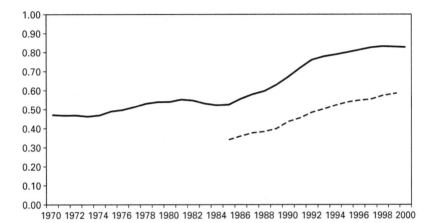

Figure I.1
Indices of structural reform in Latin America, 1970–2000, elaborated on
the basis of data from Carlos Santiso, from the UN Economic
Commission for Latin America (—), and from the Inter-American
Development Bank (---).

market neo-liberalism, the entire continent danced an
endless waltz of paradigms, changing step in time to the
topics, lessons and the consensus from the north. In the
early 1990s, the Washington Consensus enumerating the
ten commandments of economic reform necessary to
conquer underdevelopment was ultimately just another
variation on that endless waltz. As with other transplant-
ed theories, this one did not take root, and like many others it was painfully rejected by a continent that had been
continually wounded and scarred by macroeconomic
surgical interventions.

But over the course of the last two decades, a great

transformation seems to be emerging in Latin America, more subtle and fragile than a simple shift of paradigms. As indicated in figure I.1, which measures the reform effort on a scale of 0 to 1 (1 corresponds to the maximum reforms), the region's economies have propelled one of the most remarkable reform processes of their history, in tandem with a generalized movement toward democracy. Although incomplete and imperfect, this synchronized dual movement of economic reforms and a transition to democracy is very encouraging.

To a large extent, this political and economic shift has been accompanied by an epistemic change. The reform policies enacted reflect a more pragmatic approach, a political economy of the possible. The history of Latin America seems to have split at some point near the end of the twentieth century. It is true that the search for utopia still endures. The governments of many countries in the region continue to talk about magical formulas and lyric exaltations. These chimeras turn into yet more tragic realisms and painful falls, as the recent experiences of several nations, flattened by unprecedented recessions, show. The shortcuts they insist on taking in order to avoid the long and winding path of gradual reform only lead these countries into more dead ends.

But other nations, like Chile under Lagos or Brazil under Lula, strive not to invent a third way but simply to forge their own path of pragmatic political economy that combines neo-classical orthodoxies with progressive social policies. In these Latin American countries, eco-

nomic reformers are not afraid of straying from the mold
of economic paradigms. Their economic ministers and
the governors of their central banks have adopted a pragmatic spirit, in contrast to their predecessors, and without blushing have embraced the American philosopher
Richard Rorty's formula which considers "theory as an
aid to practice, rather than seeing practice as a degrada-
tion of theory."[1] These economic policies are intended to
offer hope to a continent tired of therapies consisting of
shocks and counter-shocks, of structural adjustments and
misadjustments. At the beginning of this century, the trajectories of Chile, Brazil, and Mexico outline the profile of
a great, unheralded transformation: the silent emergence
of the political economy of the possible.

Like many other world events announced with bom-
bast in the newspapers, it may be that this advent is only
temporary, and that all the fanfare will be in vain. The
Chilean experience suggests, however, that this transformation may endure. Over the past two decades, we can
see how this country patiently reworked its institutions,
examining the good and bad aspects of political regimes
and economic models. In Chile the impulses of the political elite have been moderated by the realism of the economic elite. Under Cardoso and Lula, Brazil has followed in the footsteps of its Chilean neighbor with a car-
ioca style of pragmatism. Both Chile and Brazil have
built anchors of endogenous credibility—institutions
and economic policies that are connected to the social
realities of their respective countries, not to economics

textbooks that do not pay sufficient attention to countries marked by poverty and inequality. Their leaders know that sooner or later they can be tempted to dive in without thinking, beckoned by the siren call of the politically impossible policies. Wisely, like Ulysses, they have tied themselves to the masts of fiscal and monetary institutions that they themselves have erected. Farther north, there is another example, another variation: Mexico has also created its own institutions, firmly tied to rigorous fiscal and monetary policies. However, with respect to its southern cousins, Mexico benefits from an enormous weapon in its favor, an anchor of external credibility: the country not only invents its own institutions in an endogenous manner, like its neighbors; it also has the scope to broaden these under the protection of the agreement signed in the mid-1990s with the United States. In this way, the North American Free Trade Agreement (NAFTA) acts as a powerful magnet for the convergence of nominal variables such as inflation and interest rates, as well as of institutional processes.

Two methodologies, two variations, two development strategies, sometimes combined, are taking place in Latin America: the anchor of endogenous credibility, propelled internally, and another anchor of exogenous credibility, supported externally. The challenge for many Latin American countries, however, is that they are not able to count on this type of exogenous anchor. Mexico, by virtue of its geographic location, is an exception. For other nations, the road is more arduous. They can only count on occasional support, a free trade agreement here, a bilateral agreement there, but nothing comparable to the tight embrace that has benefited Mexico since 1994. For these other countries, the strategy of an endogenous credibility anchor combined with the slow fermentation of institutions, like making a fine wine, is the only possible path. Chile, Brazil, Costa Rica, Trinidad and Tobago, Colombia, Uruguay—there is no lack of examples. There are counterexamples, of course, because in dealing with the Americas plurality must always be taken into account. Other trajectories are more erratic; for instance, those of Argentina or Venezuela, and those of Ecuador and Bolivia, testify to the region's still-powerful attraction to the sirens' song. Here and there, yesterday's Good Revolutionaries (and the Good Free-Marketeers) return in their pontoon boats and cast the rich galleons bearing economic policies that flourished long ago against the reefs of grand illusions. In Cuba, the lighthouse of an ever-present revolution continues to project its beacon. After more than 45 years in power, Fidel Castro, the longest-lasting Latin American leader still in power, displays an insolent political longevity. He has survived a dozen American presidents, Republican and Democrat, and, like a hundred-year-old patriarch from Macondo, he seems to recognize his biological end as the only temporal limit on his exercise of power.

The fits and starts of recent years attest to Latin America's continuing obsession with the idea of an all-powerful economic paradigm and with the search for a magic formula that can free it from all ailments. The great transformation outlined for some decades is nothing more than one possible reading of the region's development process. Once again today, Latin Americans find themselves at a crossroads. Beginning in 2006, Latin Americans in a number of countries will go to the polls to elect presidents. Once again they will have to choose a path between the political economy of the impossible and that which is possible. The examples of Lula in Brazil and Lagos in Chile may indicate to other countries the way to a new political economy of the possible. Good Revolutionaries and Free-Marketeers could then exit the stage, or they could return to inflame the still-hot embers of the political economy of the impossible. The history of Latin America is, like a toss of the dice, unpredictable and open to possibilities. The great news we have from Latin America is this: Open societies emerge (to paraphrase Karl Popper) politically and economically from societies that give a preferred place to the vices and the virtues of democracy and free-market principles.

1 The Unfolding Future of Latin American Utopias

Before analyzing the political economy of the possible that Latin Americans have put into practice in the last few decades, it is important to take a stroll through history. In order to understand and gauge utopianism's enduring appeal in Latin America, we must recall that the Americas were discovered at the precise instant when temporal representations and visions of the world were radically transformed—at the exact moment when the modern notion of the future emerged in Western thought.

When Columbus arrived in Hispaniola, Europe was experiencing a profound transformation of its vision of the world. In Italy, architects and painters from Brunelleschi to Piero Della Francesca were discovering perspective. The Quattrocento Renaissance was inventing the idea of spatial depth, and with it the Ideal City, at the time when the Americas were being discovered. Simultaneously, the Middle Ages' theological orientation toward time was crumbling as church bell towers gave way to the merchants' belfries and to the princes' clocks, which denoted secular time. Europe's centuries-old world vision—conditioned in part by the idea that life on Earth was "poor, nasty, brutish, and short," as Hobbes wrote in *Leviathan* (1651)—began to shift as the prospects of a better existence began to emerge. As the zeitgeist changed, the clergy began to combine their civil power with the ability to tell the time, and clocks were increasingly added to church towers.

In Italy, Machiavelli invented perspective in politics and explored the temporal dimensions of daily life. Other authors focused on what was once considered impossible by arguing that a better world was possible here on Earth. A few years after Columbus discovered America, decisive books were published that contributed to the change in the West's conception of time and of the spatial world. In one decade, three major works, powerful as swords, appeared: Erasmus's *Praise of Folly* (1509), Machiavelli's *The Prince* (completed in 1513), and Thomas More's *Utopia* (1516). These three books soon found their way to the New World. By 1515, Erasmus's work was in the library of Hernando Columbus, the Admiral's son. A Spanish translation of *The Prince* appeared in 1552. More's *Utopia* became the favorite book of Vasco de Quiroga, bishop of Michoacán.

In 1535, the year Thomas More was beheaded by order of Henry VIII, Vasco de Quiroga established missions in Santa Fé and Michoacán. Much later, and farther to the south, the utopian impetus inspired the Jesuits in

Paraguay and the French adventurer Orélie-Antoine de Tounens, who in 1861 proclaimed himself king of Araucania, a Chilean province celebrated by the poet Alonso de Ercilla. It is not surprising that More's ideas were well received and successful in Latin America. In the book, his fictional island of Utopia is discovered by Hitloden, a Portuguese navigator who was a comrade of Américo Vespucio, which suggests that Utopia was none other than the New World that had just been discovered.

But the enchantment of space quickly turned into the spell of time. Latin America's utopia was not to be sought in the region's geography but in its future—in the temporal rather than the spatial dimension. If Latin America was born at the precise moment when the world's vision was transformed, it emerged precisely when a new equilibrium between past, present, and future was being configured. It was a moment when representations of time were being transformed, and when a theological age was giving way to a teleological age. Latin America was born in what J. G. A. Pocock termed "the Machiavellian moment": the period 1494–1530. The idea took shape that the progress of history was subject to human endeavor— that the future was not something to be shaped by the will of Providence but rather something to be built with the help of Fortune, and also through the exertion of effort in both the political and the economic realm.

At the end of the Middle Ages, while Machiavelli was formulating a political perspective and a profound sense of future time, and while his contemporaries were inventing perspective in painting and the idea of spatial depth, the temporal outline of history evoked by the German philosopher Reinhart Koselleck began to emerge. The future once anticipated as the end of the world began to give way to the dawn of an age more open to the future of humankind, a time in which the present was preparation for tomorrow, when governing itself became focused on anticipating and building a future, on altering and ordering not only space but also time. Then Jean Bodin and others began to dissociate the religious account of history from the history of human progress, reducing the issue of the end of time to a matter of dates, a problem of mathematical and astronomical calculation. Galileo's contention that the Earth revolved around the Sun was a shock to the traditional system, as it displaced the primacy placed on heavenly (and, by extension, the Church's) authority. In European courts, Velázquez and other artists stopped painting images of Christ and the saints in order to concentrate on the rulers of the terrestrial world in works of art that extended perspective through the use of receding points and the play of mirrors. In his *Six Books of the Commonwealth* (1576), Bodin evoked the New World not as a physical space but as a temporal dimension to be conquered: "Utopia is not found in that vast geography of the Americas. Neither El Dorado nor the Golden Age exists. What the New World offers us is a future."

More recent Latin American discourses, from Bolívar to Chávez, have been strongly imbued with this teleological dimension, locating the Golden Age not in the past but in the future. At the start of the twentieth century, the Europeans arriving in the New World, although no longer the conquistadors of old, were still motivated by the vision of America as the promised land, a continent that held the promise of a better life and a better future. In the early nineteenth century, a Scottish scoundrel by the name of Gregor McGregor even invented a rich new territory, Poyais, which he said was located in the heart of Latin America. This speculative invention quickened London's financial pulse, set the city's investors dreaming, and led to one of the first financial crises of modern times. The Mexican (1910), Cuban (1959), and Nicaraguan (1979) revolutions were further variations of the search for a resplendent future Golden Age, continually postponed. In the same way, though less tragically, the grandiose project of economic integration on a continental scale did not cease striving toward a better future. Like an endlessly receding horizon, the promised land of continuous growth and of reduced inequality was a future that remained unrealized because it remained forever out of reach. Much revolutionary oratory, whether inspired by Marxism or monetarism, took root in this fertile ground, from which hope sprang eternal. The eloquent principles of their magnificent discourses, enveloped in ethical sensibility and intensely emotional rhetoric, contrasted sharply with their failure to materialize.

Throughout the twentieth century, the entire Latin American continent was propelled by, and at times

buffeted by, the variable winds emanating from the
"great ideological storms" that surged from the search
for the ideal.[1] All over the continent, the operative word
became "revolution," a conceptual projection that pointed to a temporal beyond simultaneously designated as a
rupture and a return. Cuban or Chilean, Marxist or
Liberal, the idea of "revolution" was sustained by the
idea of fostering a better future through sacrifices made
in the immediate present. A horizon of high expectations
was established that would enable the hopes based on
the present economic and political sacrifices eventually
to be fulfilled. From Peru's Shining Path to the exalted
lyrics of Chavismo, from Fujimorism to Menemismo, the
last two decades of the twentieth century merely prolonged this tireless and sometimes tragic search.

From the Good Revolutionary to the Good Liberal
Free-Marketeer

A short book published nearly 30 years ago by a
Venezuelan essayist perfectly captured the spirit of its
time and had great resonance. In *The Latin Americans:
Their Love-Hate Relationship with the United States*, Carlos
Rangel denounced the revolutionary mythologies and
the lyric illusions of the entire Latin American continent.
He attacked, in particular, the great leaps forward that
turned out to be yet more leaps backward, as the ill-
spent decade of the 1980s subsequently proved.
Intending to be polemic, Rangel attacked all those who

let off steam by engaging in voluntaristic and futuristic diatribes or who obscured the realities of a continent with its veins open. But above all, Rangel noted the tendency of Westerners to project their own designs upon the region, and the equally strong propensity of Latin Americans to complacently mirror an expected image of intellectual guerrillas voicing the obligatory revolutionary ideology. With the diffusion of Marxism in all its forms, Latin America, "daughter to the noble savage, wife to the good revolutionary," became the "predestined mother to the new man,"[2] a place where utopias not attainable elsewhere continued to remain possible.

Stereotypes are difficult to fight and often prosper on fertile ground. The countries of Latin America undergo change differently, taking on unexpected hues, and sometimes they shed their skins. An archaeology of contemporary political and economic knowledge still largely remains to be developed. But already the transformation of the Latin American continent is palpable. For the continent as a whole, the conceptual and practical frames of politics have changed considerably. The majority of Latin America's intellectuals and leaders have converted to market economics and to political democracy. "Democracy" and "the Market" have replaced "the Revolution" and "the State" at the altar of belief. An entire vocabulary has disappeared from political and economic discourse, allowing for the growth of a new set of ideas. Expressions such as "class warfare," "economic planning," and "import substitution strategies" have been replaced by expressions such as "democratic consensus," "institutional consolidation," "economic deregulation," and "free trade opening."

The conversion to a market-based ideology can appear problematic at first. Whether it is a question of shifting frames of reference and action or the result of convenience or conviction, this sea change is tied to an investment in values and in the reconversion of interests. In fact, we may ask ourselves whether "Democracy," perceived as a horizon of expectations in the sense Koselleck alluded to as something always strived for but continually elusive, has not been substituted for the teleological dimension of "the Revolution." In unseating "the State" as the regulator of the social and economic realms, "the Market" also has, in a way, taken its place in the totalizing tradition of Latin American thought. Have the Good Liberal Free-Marketeer and the Good Democrat supplanted the Good Savage and the Good Revolutionary?

Even more extraordinary is that in the last two decades some Latin American leaders have proven to be strange chameleons. They have draped themselves in populist hues, then dressed in clearly liberal shades the morning after election. Politically populist and economically neo-liberal, they are all chameleons who take issue with the subtle analyses of economists at the Massachusetts Institute of Technology and the World Bank or those of their colleagues at the University of Chicago and the International Monetary Fund. In textbooks, Latin American populist macroeconomics has difficulty adapting to the less tropical rigors of free-market economics. Nevertheless, in the 1990s Menem made Argentina dance a furiously neo-liberal tango. Farther to the north, Fujimorismo put Peru on a shining but precipitous path of structural adjustments. And Salinismo raised the heartbeat of the Institutional Revolutionary Party and suffocated Mexico when it accelerated the march of so-called neo-liberal economic reforms. Under Chávez, Venezuela, the last metamorphosis of this Latin American chameleon, manages to repeat the revolutionary exhortations of a past era.

From Marxism to Neo-Liberalism, or the Political Economy of the Impossible

Latin America is a region of extremes. Plagued by extreme violence and blessed by extreme beauty, it is heir to terrible injustices and poverty as well as to baroque fortunes. It is also a region that over the course of the twentieth century was subjected to great ideological pressures. Latin America has an enduring belief in a rationality that dominates the social arena and its ability to shape it.

From one decade to another, numerous ideological storms swept away the certainties of yesterday and with them the debris of barely sketched reforms. Over a period of approximately 30 years, Latin America has been deluged with paradigms and models. This tropical meteorology, with sudden cloudbursts and equally sudden clearing, was often maintained by the Latin Americans themselves. It was also often encouraged by foreign specialists, successors to the "money doctors" of the Kemmerer missions that in the 1920s gathered specialists from the social sciences to uncover the laws of change in supposedly malleable regions, comparable extensions, or gigantic sky-lit laboratories available and on offer as if they were the great copper mines that color the tip of South America.

The role of foreign advisors has, therefore, been ambivalent. Throughout the history of Latin American development, they helped to establish solid institutions—for example, the Kemmerer Mission of 1925 resulted in the founding of Chile's central bank. But foreign advisors often lacked political knowledge and often were unable to adapt theorems and formulas to the specific alchemy of the local fragile and highly volatile components of politics. The Klein-Saks Mission, for example, which helped to design and implement an anti-inflationary stabilization package in Chile in 1955–1958, played a pivotal role, bringing, as shown by Sebastián Edwards, an economic expertise, unavailable by the time in Chile, that boosted the initial credibility of the program. But providing technical economic pre-commitments was not enough to ensure success; political adoption and implementation also were important. Chile's congress failed to act decisively on the fiscal front, and the stabilization program launched in 1955 failed to achieve durable price stability. This example is, however, a benign one. The furious imposition of magical paradigms onto Latin American social and political realities was much more damaging, amplifying with its radicality the cycles of boom and bust and bringing to the region a cognitive violence that, from time to time, went hand in hand with the use of force. In fact, by the end of the twentieth century a swarm of theories and paradigms had been unleashed on the region. This theoretical "ideological escalation" or deluge of paradigms (described and denounced by Albert Hirschman in *Journeys toward Progress*) was often accompanied by extreme experiments inspired by what Hirschman called Flaubert's "rage de vouloir conclure"—that is, the impatience of thinkers affected by the compulsion to theorize, the "headlong rush toward the pseudo-insight."[3] Rigid economic models constituted yet another invitation to design radical alternatives that lacked any intermediate shades of chiaroscuro.

The liberal and democratic instincts exhibited today by many Latin American intellectuals and leaders could well be the prolongation of the tendency described above, another episode in this game of ever-shifting paradigms. Finally, might these conversions yet again illustrate the permeability and the swiftness with which the radical thoughts and ideas of others are adopted in Latin America to take the form of pseudo-creative solutions to problems? Put another way, it may merely be another illustration of this manner of considering and conducting political economy through the prism of paradigms that articulate laws of absolute change and forecast eternally radiant future horizons.

Today, the agreement and coordination between the region's agents and observers underscores the extent to which Latin America's conceptual universe has been transformed over the last 30 years—say, since the publication of Rangel's book. At that time, "the Revolution" and "the State" were the unavoidable concepts littering the ideological landscape, and every good Latin American then alive was, in thought, action, and speech, a Good Revolutionary. Similarly, in the economic sphere, the development of the region was inconceivable without the support of the State, the insuperable engine and agent of growth. In that earlier period, "Democracy" was always adjectivized conceptually and instrumentalized politically as "formal" or "armed"; the left thought of it as an instrument and the right as a subterfuge. Cuban or Chilean, social or neo-liberal, revolution was the matrix conveying the vision of the Latin American universe and the prism through which the rest of the world saw and wanted to see this region. Later, economic liberalization and political democratization made inroads, bringing with them an entirely new vocabulary and a new grammar of political economy whose alphabet consistently spelled out "the Market" and "Democracy."

2 The Present Decline: Latin America in the Garden of Democratic Delights

Tocqueville speculated that a political regime as delicate as the one that prospered in the United States would not acclimate itself to the hemisphere's more tropical zones.[1] From north to south, however, democracy has taken root throughout the Americas, refuting the predictions of the author of *Democracy in America*. In Costa Rica and in Uruguay, the democratic tradition established itself early in exemplary ways. In Uruguay, democracy took root in the late 1820s. In Costa Rica, it has been in place since the beginning of the twentieth century, albeit with a social-democratic European touch. The fate of democracy in other Latin American countries, intermittent and prone to numerous long periods of authoritarianism, has followed Tocqueville's predictions.

Despite these democratic examples, between 1950 and 1990 the majority of Latin American countries were dictatorships about two-thirds of the time, democracies about one-third of the time. But during this same period the world as a whole, and Latin America in particular, experienced a remarkable surge in the growth of democracy. In 1950, only eight of the eighteen Latin American countries could be described as democracies; 40 years later, fourteen of them could. During the same period, Latin America experienced great instability. Of the 141 countries analyzed by Adam Przeworski and his collaborators,[2] only 41 underwent de facto transitions from dictatorship to democracy. In Latin America, the rotation of political regimes was more intense during the same period. Of the 97 regime transitions catalogued, 44 took place in Latin America. In Latin America the ratio of transition was 2.4 per country during this period. It was 1.6 in Southeast Asia, and 1.2 in South Asia; in the remaining regions, it was below 1.

Latin America was also the area of the world that underwent the most transitions to democracy, a trend that accelerated greatly beginning in 1983. Since that year, none of the region's countries has experienced a political regime change, in spite of seven military insurrections and attempted coups (three in Venezuela, two in Argentina, one each in Peru and Ecuador). After democracy returned, no Latin American president was forcibly removed from office by a military insurrection. Two of the eleven interruptions of presidencies (that of Brazil's Collor in 1992 and that of Ecuador's Bucarán in 1997) followed procedures similar to the impeachment process conducted in the United States. Others presidencies ended because of videos revealing the machinations of corruption, or as a consequence of broad popular peaceful protests (Fujimori in Peru and Mahuad in Ecuador, respectively, both in 2000; Gutiérrez in Ecuador in 2005 in response to popular protests; Carlos Mesa in Bolivia in 2005). The rest voluntarily relinquished their power after massive protests degenerated into significant disturbances: the 1989 street uprisings in Buenos Aires over the hyperinflation that Alfonsín's government was unable to stop, and again in 2001 to dislodge De la Rúa, paralyzed by the dimensions of the Argentine crisis; in Caracas against the corruption of Carlos Andrés Pérez's government, and also in Paraguay.

In fact, the old dictators and revolutionaries themselves—putting down their weapons, as Bolivia's Banzer and Nicaragua's Ortega did—continued to appear on ballots throughout the 1990s and the 2000s. When Hugo Chávez, a former army officer who calls himself a socialist revolutionary, was first elected Venezuela's president in 1998, he defeated the opposition in nine successive ballots, and he is expected to win reelection in the presidential contest of late 2006. In Brazil, Latin America's largest democracy, the people elected as their president Luiz Inácio Lula da Silva, a former metalworker, born in poverty, who rose from shoeshine boy to trade-union leader and founder of the Partido dos Trabalhadores (PT), the largest left-wing force in Latin America. Brazilian leaders, headed by Fernando Henrique Cardoso, made the 2002 transfer of power a master lesson in political elegance that was the envy of their elder democratic brothers in the developed countries.

In the last two decades, Latin America's democracies
have multiplied. In the early 1980s, disenchantment with
revolutionary utopians merged with the aura from the
Spanish and the Portuguese democratic transitions, giving credit to the idea that democracy is possible in Latin
countries. Amid disenchantment with the utopian vision
and the rediscovered virtues of democracy, the debt crisis
that exploded in 1982 quickly plunged the region into a
long decade of lost growth. For a long time Latin
America's debt crisis called into question the legitimacy
of the numerous military regimes that were then in
power, while at the same time undermining the already
fragile legitimacy of populist governments. One after
another, in Argentina or Uruguay, the military regimes
tumbled like dominoes. In some instances the demise
was precipitated by a military disaster, such as
Argentina's Falklands War with Britain, then under
Margaret Thatcher's government. From one Latin
American country to another, each of the transitions produced its own democratic variant. Some were the result
of Spanish-style pacts, like the Pactos de la Moncloa conducted by the soft-liners of Spanish government and
oppositions after the death of Franco in the mid 1970s.
Others were granted by the autocrats in power or forced
by national and international pressures. In 1989, the year
when the Chilean democrats came to power and the
Berlin Wall fell, the cycle of the great Latin American
transitions in the southernmost region of the continent
came to a close. In 2000, the Mexican electorate, long

enthralled by the delights of democracy, took a new direction and, for the first time in nearly 70 years of uninterrupted power held by the Partido Revolucionario Institucional, elected an opposition candidate not from the PRI: Vicente Fox, a former Coca-Cola executive and governor from the small state of Guanajuato who emerged from the center-right and had the backing of the Partido de Acción Nacional.

Since the democratization wave, an army of specialists has directed its attention to examining the significant democratic turn in Latin America. Their debates have generated tons of paper and have led to entire subgenres in the literature on development: "transitology" and then, once democratic regimes were established, "consolidology." An army of "transitologists" attempted to translate these concepts into political realities. By disentangling the web of facts, they aspired to deduce from them the laws, logic, and order from which to create a theoretical body of implacable axioms and norms interchangeable from one country to another. But, in a way, we have witnessed the failure of transitology. The search for the economic, social, and cultural determinants of the laws governing democratic change were effectively and considerably revised, reaching greater indeterminacy, and taking into consideration the complications introduced by the actors' decisions and the uncertain conditions. Thus, there is now more fragmented thinking favoring a relatively modest conceptual theory that invites a healthy dose of humility. Above all, this body of literature attests to an epistemological change. Studies concentrating on the preconditions as structural and determining elements of these democratizations were followed by studies proposing the primacy of the strategies, decisions, and preferences of actors. This shift in focus resulted in the modification of temporal coordinates of the processes under analysis. Works inspired by sociology, propelled by winds from the past, and focused on structural matters gave way to works inspired by economics, looking toward the future, and conceding a more important place to the effects of immediately relevant policy measures. Implicitly or explicitly, these game-theory-inspired analyses integrate assessments favored by economists that focus on possible or likely future outcomes arising from actions taken in the immediate present. These newer studies, which have turned into genuine exercises that have reversed the direction of time, are concerned with potential scenarios viewed not from the vantage point of the past (structures, conditions, and determining factors) but rather from the future (opportunities, actions, and consequences).

One of the most notable developments in the investigations of the turn to democracy turns on a radical questioning of the illusions inherent in retrospective rationalizations and the nature of determinism. The causal linearity of democratic processes, the sequential and chronological chain of events, has been seriously questioned. Certainly neither Juan Linz nor Adam Przeworski, the authors of the most outstanding analyses of the phenomena of democratization (respectively in 1978 and 1991) nor many other political scientists have renounced the legitimate practice of attempting to separate weak from strong moments in order to document the march of events and how these logically interact. But according to these specialists, democratizations are not linear processes that have occurred in a completely determined and irreversible manner; instead they are like grains of sand in an hourglass. The images of a clock's pendulum and its balancing oscillations would be more appropriate metaphors to describe these tentative and unstable democratic trajectories than linear constructions.

Ultimately, the story of these democratizations was the chronicle of the death foretold of authoritarianism, rather than a narrative structure identical to that of two diverging garden paths that take random tangents and turns, as in Jorge Luis Borges's short story *The Garden of Forking Paths* or Paul Auster's novel *The Music of Chance*, with unexpected consequences and hidden luck forming the story's intrigue. The transformation of the temporal coordinates being analyzed in the democratization process also responded to the echoing transformation of time altered by political reality. The broad temporal horizons of the autocrats were followed by the shorter temporalities of democracy, political life being delimited by electoral terms and mandates. Following the rhythm of the electoral calendars, the political agendas of democrats were also under the temporal empire of opinion polls and of the news media. In Latin America, history has crowned the time of democracy par excellence; that is, present time. In this sense, one can speak about a narrowing of temporal horizons or about a shortened time frame. The skillful management of time in itself constitutes a fundamental variable in the success or failure of the democratization process. The political economy of transitions and democratic consolidations is, above all, a matter of timing, of arbitrating intertemporal compromises between immediate and future victories. Put another way, it is a matter of skillfully balancing immediate pressures and imperatives against future expectations and probabilities. It is, above all, about remedying what is most urgent, a timing device or, on the contrary, a matter of accelerating reforms, delineating agendas, and resolving the consequences.

Beyond these temporal transformations of political timing, the most significant event at the conclusion of the twentieth century was the fact that democracy took root in Latin American soil and endured politically. It is true that in 2005 many of the region's democracies had barely celebrated their twentieth anniversary, but, though still in their political adolescence, these regimes seem to be durable. It is worth noting that, in spite of the widespread and recurring financial crises that Latin America has suffered in the last decade, the popular preference for democracy has not diminished. According to a 2003 poll by Latinobarómetro, a Chile-based polling firm that coordinates large surveys throughout the region, the principal countries that claimed a strongly democratic preference included precisely those nations that had suffered the worst economic recessions of their contemporary history. In Uruguay and in Argentina, where gross domestic product (GDP) fell by nearly 11 percent in 2002 (a 100-year record for both countries), support for democracy continued to be firm the following year, with 2003 preference rates for democracy of 78 percent and 68 percent, respectively. In Venezuela, the recessions of 2002 and 2003 (at an annual GDP decline of approximately 9 percent, also a record since the 1930s) and the rise of Chavismo (the revolution led by Chávez in Venezuela, mixing Marxism with populism and nationalism) have strengthened support for democracy instead of eroding it. In these three countries, the preference for democracy did not waver under the pressure of economic crises; it did so only by a few points in the cases of Argentina and Uruguay and even grew in the case of Venezuela. Similarly, and in a more general manner, although opinion polls undeniably reveal a disenchantment with democracy, in two-thirds of countries the level of satisfaction with democracy has risen, in spite of years of modest economic growth and sometimes great shocks and financial crises. This advance confirms that the citizens of Latin America increasingly distinguish between democracy as a political system and the accomplishments of the economic goals announced by democratic governments.

The polls mentioned above also corroborate the existence of an uneven erosion in the preference for democracy. But the ambivalence of the responses is sometimes due to the questions posed. If the question allows for nuances and centers on the statement that democracy may suffer from problems but is the best system of government, 64 percent of Latin Americans would ratify Churchill's edict. This preference is manifest in the region's "old" democracies (Costa Rica), in the countries with an extensive democratic past (Uruguay), as well as in the "young" democracies (Mexico). The data from the 2004 polls showed that, despite the crises, the growing dissatisfaction and disillusionment with their political leaders, 72 percent of Latin Americans continued to believe that democracy is the only political system that can contribute to economic development. An even more remarkable fact is that this bet on democracy, as in the previous poll, reached its highest rate in the three economies most harshly punished by the crises: Venezuela (where 86 percent of the population shares this opinion), Uruguay (84 percent), and Argentina (79 percent).

There is a strong likelihood that democracy will continue in the region. Over the period 1950–1990, if we add the total number of years lived under each type of political regime in the eighteen Latin American countries, dictatorship and democracy are split relatively evenly: the countries of Latin America amassed 372 years of life under dictatorships and 366 years under democracies. But if we include the years 1990–2006, the equilibrium clearly favors democracy. Latin American countries thus accumulated more than 600 years of life under democra-

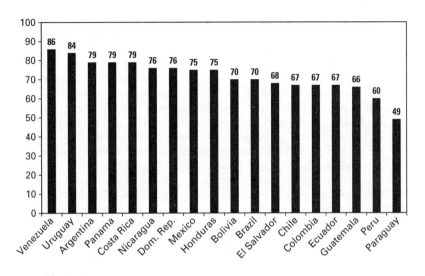

Figure 2.1
Percentage of responses affirming the statement "Democracy is the only political system that can help the development of the country." Source: Santiso 2005, based on 2004 Latinobarómetro polls.

cy, versus 400 years under dictatorship. In fact, for the eighteen countries analyzed during the period 1978–2006, the average longevity of democracy is 23 years. (See table 2.1.) Following the taxonomy established by Przeworski, if we take into account that the years 1950, 1958, and 1959 corresponded to the establishment of democratic presidencies in Costa Rica, Colombia, and Venezuela respectively, the average lifespan of the region's democratic regimes was actually greater than 26 years. This attractive temporal arithmetic, however, shows some cracks. In recent years, specialists have been

Table 2.1
Lifespans of democratic regimes in Latin America since 1978. Source: Santiso 2005, updated on the bases of data from the Inter-American Development Bank. Note: Colombia, Costa Rica, and Venezuela elected their leaders through democractic processes long before 1978. For those countries, the reference year used below corresponds to the year when the study began. As we have already noted, if we consider that the years of the definitive establishment of democracy in these countries are the decades of the 1940s and 1950s, these three countries exhibit an uninterrupted half-century of democratic life. For Mexico there are various possible dates which have been the subject of debate in the analyses: the year 1982 corresponds to the bridge year in which the country started important constitutional and economic changes propelled by President Miguel de la Madrid. There are also other possible years: 1988, the year in which especially disputed and polemical elections took place; 1994, when Ernesto Zedillo took office, or also 2000, the year in which power shifted with the arrival of opposition leader Vicente Fox.

	Year of transition	Years of democracy
Colombia	1978	28
Costa Rica	1978	28
Dominican Republic	1978	28
Ecuador	1979	27
Venezuela	1979	27
Peru	1980	26
Bolivia	1982	24
Honduras	1982	24
Mexico	1982	24
Argentina	1983	23
El Salvador	1984	22
Uruguay	1985	21
Guatemala	1985	21
Brazil	1985	21
Panama	1989	17
Paraguay	1989	17
Chile	1990	16
Nicaragua	1990	16
Mean		23

concerned by these adolescent democracies. Hyper-presidentialism, "decretism" (meaning the executive use—and sometime abuse—of decrees to curb parliamentary rule), delegated democracy, or even low-intensity democracy: there is no absence of qualifying terms to denounce the disturbances to the growth of the region's democracies. For some countries, the diagnosis is cautious, and clearly more favorable for others, since the clinical condition of democracy varies from one country to the next. But an overall confirming trend is apparent in the region as a whole: as happened in the old democracies, the citizens' dissatisfaction with respect to their leaders has increased. The Pan-American annual polls of Latinobarómetro corroborate this: between 1996 and 2003, satisfaction decreased considerably. In all countries, with the exception of Venezuela, satisfaction with democracy has receded. Above all, this dissatisfaction refers to the economic achievements of the democratic regime. In other words, people vote with their wallets according to a leader's ability to take the country on the path to growth, and not only as a preference for democracy as such, as mentioned previously. There has been a peak in this dissatisfaction; the level of Latin Americans satisfied with the functioning of their democracies fell to 28 percent in 2003 from 53 percent in 1996. In another sense, this dissatisfaction can also be interpreted positively, as proof of citizen's greater political maturity. But this erosion is uneven, and a more detailed analysis allows the introduction of certain nuances. In fact, other polls indicate that the democratic preference is taking root in Latin America. According to the World Values Survey which took place between 1995 and 2000 under the direction of Pippa Norris and Ronald Inglehart, 96 percent of Uruguayans believe that democracy is the best political system (a greater percentage than is found among Swedes or Norwegians). The percentage is 86 percent for Peruvians (the same as that among Spaniards), 85 percent for Argentines (the same as that among Americans), 83 percent among Brazilians, 77 percent among Chileans, and 65 percent among Mexicans. On average, more than 80 percent of Latin Americans approve of democratic ideals, a conviction in tune with the global average. Disenchantment can be read, however, when citizens are asked about the accomplishments of democracy: the average rate of satisfaction does not exceed 62 percent, compared to 68 percent in the case of Europe's older democracies.

The slowdown of incoming leaders' popularity has sometimes reached record levels. In a matter of a couple of months, the popularity of certain newly elected presidents has dropped sharply. For instance, Alejandro Toledo in Peru saw his popularity decrease drastically in less than a year after coming into office, and drop below 10 percent midway through his term. He survived with this minimalist approval rate until the 2006 presidential elections. Peru's example is significant because of the speed at which the power of the government vanished. It illustrates, likewise, how that erosion can at times be dis-

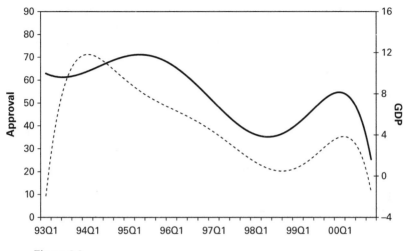

Figure 2.2
Approval of Fujimori in polls (—) and change in GDP (---), 1993–2000.
Source: BBVA Banco Continental.

connected from macroeconomic growth. Contrary to
what took place at the end of Fujimori's government,
when the deteriorating economic situation fomented
political unrest, none of this happened in Toledo's case:
in spite of a booming economy, his approval rates continued to dive, one more recurring proof that Peruvians differentiate between the economic and political spheres
without establishing systematic causal relations. The paradox is that Toledo managed to finish his term, whereas
Fujimori fled Peru before the end of his term because of
corruption scandals.

The speed of the erosion of popular support presents a
great challenge for emerging new democracies. If we take

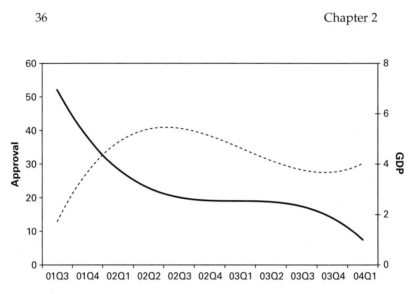

Figure 2.3
Approval of Toledo in (—) and change in GDP (---), 2001–2004. Source:
BBVA Banco Continental.

into account that the capacity to enact reforms is concentrated largely in the first months of government, the
famous hundred days of grace, the rapidity at which the
legitimacy of leaders and their ability to govern erodes is
problematic, especially in countries in which the imperative for reforms accumulates.

On closer examination, one can observe two large
groups of countries: those in which a plethora of electoral
promises were made by the new leaders, and those in
which, on the contrary, the promises were much more
moderate. In Chile, Mexico, Brazil, and Colombia, because
of promises contained or acted upon, the popularity of the
presidents has stayed high (even just after 2005 corruption

scandals, Lula's popularity stood at 60 percent). In Peru, Ecuador, Bolivia, and other countries, the lyrical overflow of the political campaigns and the flourishing of promises that could not be fulfilled provoked vertiginous declines in the popularity of the recently elected presidents. The short honeymoons were proportional to the lyrical impetus of the prenuptial campaigns.

Even so, these background tendencies illustrate the arrival of maturity in some countries' democratic regimes. In many of these countries, the threshold of the population's tolerance with respect to government corruption has decreased noticeably, and through the media Latin American societies are questioning these practices that citizens want to ban from their republics. In the same way, the votes to punish those leaders who do not achieve economic goals have become more systematic, and voters evaluate those accomplishments retrospectively. In this way, the prospective voters, who judge and weigh the political economy of the outgoing government based on the promises of politicians seeking election, are added to the count. The price of the entry ticket seems to have gone up from this point on, and to be getting closer to the practices rooted in other Western democracies. In fact, during the 1990s no outgoing Latin American government was able to continue in power once annual inflation exceeded 15 percent. Since 1983, only one Latin American government whose economy was sliding toward recession could remain in power. As the studies undertaken by Eduardo Lora and his collaborators for a

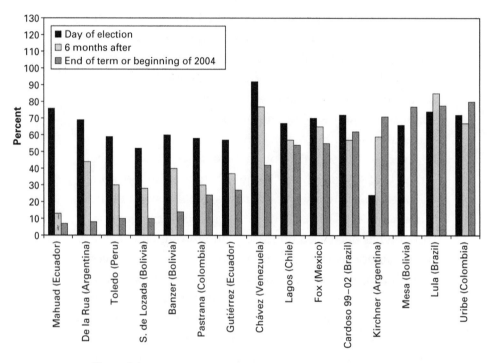

Figure 2.4
Approval of Latin American presidents. Source: Santiso 2005; based on
data from national and international polling organizations.

group of 17 countries in the region during the period 1985–2002 (67 presidential elections and 82 legislative elections) found, the Latin American electorate showed itself to be particularly sensitive to the accomplishments and failures of their leaders in matters of economic growth and inflation.

Democracy, or Consecration of the Present

An even more fundamental question for the emerging Latin American democracies concerns democracy's temporal horizons. There are 1,001 definitions of democracy. Undoubtedly one of the most relevant is the one offered by the political scientist Juan Linz, who defines democracy as government pro tempore. Democratic leaders are temporary depositories of power, since their terms have clearly defined time limits. From this point of view, by virtue of the temporality of its limited horizon, democracy is different than autocracy and dictatorship. In autocratic regimes, leaders seek, on the contrary, to prolong their power and to excuse themselves from the political time limits that are imposed in democracies. Citizens in democracies willingly subject themselves to these time limits, and take care to respect the tempos set by regular and recurrent elections. Like the Patriarch of Macondo invented by the Colombian writer Gabriel García Márquez, the autocrats dream of suspending time and aspire to remain in power unless obligated to leave by old age or death.

One of the difficulties in democracies, nevertheless, is
how to limit the undesirable effects of reduced time horizons. As the works of Mancur Olson and even those of
Douglass North and his collaborators show, when leaders' terms are limited, the temptation to despoil while in
power is greater. To ameliorate this perverse effect and to
limit this propensity, either the horizons must necessari-
ly become indefinite (which is impossible by definition in
a democratic regime) or the system must generate its
own checks and balances—that is, institutions that force
governments with limited time horizons to act as though
they had infinite horizons at their disposal. The history of
the development of financial institutions illustrates this
imperative perfectly. As the works of Stephen Haber and
his collaborators show, only structural measures and
incentives stimulating institutional policy limits that
curb the government's despoiling tendencies permit
financial systems to prosper; Haber's argument is illustrated by the history of the banking systems developed in
the United States and Mexico at the beginning of the
twentieth century.

Mexico's experiences also confirm this need for a
defensive barricade. In the 1990s, in the wake of the
nationalization of the early 1980s, Mexico experienced
two major bank reforms. In 1991, during the first of these
reforms, Mexican authorities privatized the banking
system, with the goal of raising the offer prices to the
maximum and therefore the revenue derived from selling activities. The combination of a weak normative

body and the absence of institutions capable of guaranteeing rigorous supervision of ex-ante risks and ex-post property rights led to poor lending practices. When the country experienced episodes of strong financial turbulence in 1994, the earlier reform led, less than 4 years after it was launched, to a financial crisis whose cost is estimated at more than $65 billion. The second experience, which began in 1997, consisted of reforming the system and allowing the inflow of foreign banks expected to bring with them not only cash but also technological platforms and more rigorous risk management tools. For their part, the Mexican authorities created more rigorous bank supervision in tandem with increasing the independence of the central bank, an institution that in time became one of the most credible and respected in Latin America.

Another difficulty, typical of emerging democracies, is rooted in the tight time constraints with respect to the dynamics of reforms. While the calls of the first generation are often for rapid development, because the expense of privatization and the reduction of tariff barriers occurs almost immediately, the second generation calls for reforms that mature more slowly. Therefore, there is a legitimate desire on the part of Latin American leaders (although in some cases this simply disguises the wish to stay in power) to be reelected in order to harvest and enjoy the fruits of their reform efforts. There is also a certain "political economy of impatience" on the part of these executives, which consists in forcing the approval of laws or legally extending the time horizons of their mandates. Finally, there is the proliferation, in some extreme cases, of assaults on the leaders in power, legislative changes, the multiplication of decrees, and political pressures at the margins of legal limits—what some call (with exaggeration) micro-breakdowns in democracy. Over the past two decades, 120 assaults of this type have been confirmed, encompassing 45 percent of the time that has elapsed since these countries' return to democracy. With the exception of Chile, all have experienced this deteriorating type of democratic tension. In Peru and Colombia this encompasses nearly 90 percent of the total time period since 1980, in Ecuador nearly 60 percent, Brazil and Venezuela each about 40 percent, and in Argentina 30 percent. This type of analysis, however, misses the essence, which is that no macro-democratic breakdowns have been registered since the return to democracy in the last wave of democratizations. The time when democratic regimes in Latin America were doomed to fail has been left decidedly in the past. Since 1950, more than 70 coups d'états have been documented (of which 25 were against the military), but their frequency decreased dramatically in the 1980s and practically disappeared in the 1990s.

Beyond these extreme cases, attempts to acknowledge the time needed to effect economic reforms have multiplied in emerging democracies. In the last decade, constitutional reforms authorizing reelection have proliferated as leaders have attempted to reconcile the brief periods of democracy and the longer times necessary to effect reform. Fujimori in Peru in 1993 and in 1994 Menem in Argentina and Cardoso in Brazil all obtained constitutional amendments that authorized their immediate reelections. In 2005, Colombia opted for an analogous arrangement authorizing Alvaro Uribe to seek a second term in 2006. Today, approximately two-thirds of Latin American political regimes allow a president to run for a second term, either immediately following the first one or after a set period of time. In the past two decades, ten countries have modified their legislation in this respect, and all except Paraguay have done so in order to bring about an immediate reelection, or one after a period of transition.

As a general rule, the majority of Latin American countries now have 4-year presidential terms, with the possibility of immediate reelection. But the length of presidential terms, with an average of 5 years, also has been modified. Of a total of 18 countries studied, eight elect their presidents for a 4-year term, seven for 5 years, and three for 6 years. Seven countries have modified the term of the mandates, generally in order to lengthen them, but also to shorten them with the possibility of reelection. When mandates are longer, as in Chile or Mexico (6 years—note, however, that in 2005 Chile reduced the term to 4 years with no immediate re-election possible) or Uruguay, Paraguay, Panama, Nicaragua, El Salvador, and Bolivia (5 years), immediate reelection has been rejected. In this respect, the exceptions are Peru and Venezuela, with terms of 5 and 6 years respectively, with the possibility of immediate reelection. In this way, a president can—in theory—maintain his power continuously for a total of 12 years in Venezuela, 10 years in Peru, and 8 years in Brazil and Argentina.

Przeworski's calculations and those of his collaborators for the period 1950–1990 confirm that actual time spent in power by democratic heads of state is, however, less than the average duration of electoral mandates. Chief executives stay in power an average of 3.5 years, and presidents of democracies barely reach 4 years. Dictators, for their part, appear to stay in power nearly 7.5 years. (See table 2.2.)

Another possible approach to adapting the brief duration of the presidential terms to the urgency of the reforms consists of accelerating the speed of approval and the execution of laws by allowing leaders to use emergency decrees to avoid the slowness inherent in negotiations, commissions, and special parliamentary sessions. In Peru, for example, the frenzy of emergency decrees reached a zenith during the first 2 years of Alberto Fujimori's first term, the most crucial years regarding structural reforms. During that period, more than 70 percent of the laws passed were put in place through mechanisms that allowed the compression of time. During the governments of Fernando Belaúnde (1980–1985), Alan García (1985–1990), and Valentín Paniagua (2000–2001), and during the first 4 years of the mandate of Alejandro Toledo, the same ratio did not exceed an average of 40 percent. Over the entire Fujimori period (1990–2000), it was 60 percent.

Another significant example is Argentina. After that country's return to democracy, in 1983, Raúl Alfonsín used this constitutional mechanism with moderation. But the ascension to power of the Peronist Carlos Menem in 1989 brought a spectacular loss of control of the political machinery. In less than 4 years, more than 300 emergency decrees were approved—more than 10 times the number of such decrees approved throughout Argentina's entire constitutional history between 1853 and 1989.

Latin America's democrats attempt to accommodate the tensions democracy brings with it. But electoral calendars aside, leaders of the region's democracies also should adapt, as in other parts of the world, to the power of the mass media. Hungry for real-time polling, journalists impose their rhythm on the political life of the country. One of the challenges for the leaders of emerging democracies consists in placating that furor for the present and for immediacy. Not only are they subject to the calendars of electoral terms, but the frequency of opinion polls places them under the temporal yoke of constant scrutiny. The scarcer the accomplishments in terms of growth and the distribution of wealth, the more impatient citizens feel for the concrete effects of reforms. Leaders and the led find themselves trapped by the famous "tunnel effect" evoked by Albert Hirschman,[3] an effect that leads citizens to endure (or not) an unsatisfactory present with a view to a better future. For leaders,

Table 2.2
Presidential terms and possibilities of reelection in Latin America in 2005. (X indicates availability.) Source: Santiso 2005; based on data gathered by Inter-American Development Bank.

	Term	Former term	Year changed	Immediate reelection	Non-immediate reelection	Reelection prohibited	Year changed
Argentina	4	6	1994	X			1994
Bolivia	5	4	1994		X		
Brazil	4	5	1994	X			1997
Chile	6; later 4	8	1993–2005		X		
Colombia	4	4				X	1991
Costa Rica	4	4				X	
Ecuador	4	4			X		1996
El Salvador	5	5			X		
Guatemala	4	4	1993			X	
Honduras	4	4				X	
Mexico	6	6				X	
Nicaragua	5	6	1994		X		1995
Panama	5	5			X		
Paraguay	5	5				X	1992
Peru	5	5		X			1993
Dominican Republic	4	4			X		1994
Uruguay	5	5			X		
Venezuela	6	5	1999	X			1998

the game of democracy consists in the art of temporizing. They have to manage removing themselves from impatient expectations, yet striving at the same time to extend the temporal horizon of the electorate in order to avoid their shift to other leaders if dissatisfied, their protest through negative ratings in the polls, or their punishing votes. The arts of patience, intertemporal tradeoffs, and even negotiating impatience emerge as absolute necessities in the political economy of Latin America's apprentice democracies.

In some cases, however, impatience triumphs. Protests broaden, even resulting in the overthrow of leaders, a fact confirmed by the forced ouster of Argentina's president Fernando de la Rúa in 2001, the fall of Bolivia's Sánchez de Losada in 2003, and the defeat of Ecuador's Gutiérrez in April 2005. Bolivia's Carlos Mesa was driven out of office in June 2005 after weeks of escalating protests demanding nationalization of the country's natural gas resources. Mesa quit the presidency amid debilitating protests, led by the Socialist Bolivian Indian Evo Morales, against the perceived stranglehold that transnational corporations had on Bolivia's economy. The protestors were also fighting to strip power from a political elite they felt was in bed with the transnationals—particularly from the so-called *vendepatrias* (corrupt officials willing to sell Bolivia's gas on the cheap). In other cases, this impatience has been reflected in the institutional short circuits orchestrated by the leaders themselves: when, close to exhausting all options, they can no longer act within the existing institutions, they simply import institutions. We have seen how Argentina, in the 1990s, invented a monetary fiction: the famous convertibility which assured that one Argentine peso was the equivalent of one U.S. dollar. In other countries cornered by Argentine financial crises, leaders have, nonetheless, adopted the dollar as their national currency (Ecuador and El Salvador in 2001). Instead of allowing endogenous institutions to mature slowly (and with great difficulty), they prefer to import an exogenous monetary institution—the dollar.

In other Latin American nations, dollarization continues to be important. Bank deposits in dollars amount to more than 50 percent of all deposits in countries as varied as Paraguay, Nicaragua, Peru, and Bolivia. In Uruguay, dollar deposits approached 90 percent. This dollarization, which clearly demonstrates the monetary preference of a country, constitutes an indicator of the lack of confidence in a national institution as fundamental as its currency. In certain cases, the lack of confidence is not focused on a few institutions but rather extends to all of them. Capital flight, for example, reflects citizens' generalized lack of trust in their own countries. According to Argentina's official sources, the funds owned by Argentines outside their country approached $105 billion in 2005, a sum equivalent to 75 percent of Argentina's GDP or six times the existing reserves of the central bank.

Studies of political economy focusing on the economic achievements of democracy reveal that democracy and the rule of law are closely and positively linked to economic achievements. They show that autocracies are born, die, or, on the contrary, endure, whatever the per-capita wealth, invalidating the premises of modernization theories according to which economic development makes the transition to democracy inevitable. The survival ratio of a democracy tends, on the contrary, to increase with the level of economic development and to be more sensitive to the economic achievements measured in terms of growth. Democracies have a greater tendency to decline at times of economic crisis, and presidential democracies of the Latin American kind even more so than their parliamentary equivalents. During times of growth, a parliamentary regime can hope to last 80 years. Its life expectancy drops to 26 years when the economy stalls. For presidential regimes, life expectancy is reduced from 27 years when the economy grows to barely 8 years when it declines.

We also know that democracies become particularly resilient beyond certain levels of per-capita income and certain minimal advances in educational levels. Democratic consolidation is undoubtedly related to educational improvements. Studies of the relationship between democracy and growth point in this direction and insist upon the fundamental dimension of human capital development in its dual sense as a source of growth and democratic consolidation. The countries that emerge from poverty are, after all, those that accumulate physical and human capital; they become richer and improve, and consequently, so do their institutions. One institution especially favorable to economic development, is the legal realm, as Roberto Rigobón and Dani Rodrik have pointed out.[4] Latin America has broad avenues to travel to display its reforms, less spectacular without a doubt than those first generation reforms, but equally necessary to the region's development.

All these results indicate some of the possible paths for future development in Latin America. Economic growth accompanied by a more equal distribution of income and higher levels of education, fiscal, and institutional anchorings, as well as a move toward parliamentarism rather than presidentialism, constitute the foundation stones for anchoring the future of Latin America's emerging democracies. From now on, the region will display a beautiful democratic history that belies the prophecies of Tocqueville. The movement toward democracy in the period 1945–2006 was one of the most intense in the world. It took place, in addition, amid an especially unstable international context, if we consider that international financial crises were twice as numerous after 1945 than before 1914, in the era of the first great globalization.

With respect to the standards of emerging countries, Latin America was a particularly unstable region from a political point of view. Over 35 percent of all the world's political transitions that occurred during this period were concentrated in Latin America, although it represents only 10 percent of the total number of countries. In the region as well as outside of it, the search for a better world faces a double stabilization imperative, political and economic. The region has not spared efforts in this area and has multiplied, in the past decade, its attempts at stabilization. A very broad, as well as frequently incomplete and painful, program of structural adjustments has begun, in order to synchronize its clock with the schedules and with the watchworks of the developed world, timepieces whose two hands are democracy and market economy. If the turn toward democracy constitutes one of the great stories of the past two decades, the other, equally important, points clearly to anchoring a market economy in a region which, until now, has struggled with the high and low tides of the great ideological oceans, controlled by old macropopulist or new neo-liberal moons.

3   Structural Adjustments as Temporal Adjustments

Stereotypes about Latin America's economy are recurrent. One of the most recent and tenacious is that of a region whose body and soul has been turned over to neo-liberal deities that blindly espouse market dogmas. History teaches us, however, that this neo-liberal passion, as spontaneous as it is ephemeral, conceals a subtler reality, but one that is vulnerable to being reduced to a simple paradigm shift trading the suit worn by yesterday's Good Revolutionary for that worn by the Free-Market Neo-Liberal.

Another stereotype applied to Latin America makes reference to its macroeconomic instability, with booms of spectacular growth followed by equally dramatic recessions and crises. Compared to Asia, the economies of Latin American have suffered, on average, 50 percent more crises during the period 1970–1995. The region not only suffers from crises at twice the average rate, but these crises are three times more intense than those experienced by their Asian counterparts. These sharp differences are mitigated, however, when the last decade of the twentieth century, marked by the Asian financial crisis and the search for macroeconomic stabilization in Latin America, is included in the calculation.

In fact, the volatility of growth in Latin America is particularly elevated. Over the course of the twentieth century, this volatility in annual growth reached a level of 8 percent in countries as diverse as Chile and Venezuela, with Cuba achieving a record level of 15 percent. During the twentieth century, however, this volatility has diminished, as confirmed by the example of Argentina, where annual fluctuations in GDP averaged 8 percent between 1900 and 1913 and went down to 5.4 percent between 1981 and 1996. When we compare the 1980s and the 1990s, the yearly volatility in GDP has been reduced to a moderate average of between 3.5 and 4.5 percent. Some countries have even experienced spectacular drops in macroeconomic volatility. If we consider Latin America's seven main economies (ranked by nominal GDP), namely Mexico, Brazil, Argentina, Venezuela, Colombia, Chile, and Peru, the frequency of crises has been reduced by nearly two-thirds, from a total of 26 crises in the 1980s to 9 in the following decade. (See table 3.1.)

That doesn't mean that the data we manage today have ceased having impressive yearly fluctuations. To cite only one spectacular case, Argentina experienced successive annual growth rates that went from –11 percent in 2002 to 9 percent in 2003 and again in 2004, a 20-point differential in an extremely short period of time. Just as there has been no dearth of abrupt recessions in

Table 3.1

Macroeconomic volatility in Latin America (standard deviations of rate of growth per decade). Based on 2004 data from Inter-American Development Bank and World Bank.

	1980s	1990s
Haiti	2.9	6.4
Peru	8.4	5.2
Argentina	5.6	5.5
Venezuela	4.8	5
Dominican Republic	2.7	4.4
Mexico	4.4	3.6
Chile	6.4	3.5
Ecuador	4.5	3.4
Colombia	1.5	3.3
Brazil	4.6	3
Uruguay	6.6	2.8
Panama	6.5	2.6
Honduras	2.5	2.5
Costa Rica	4.5	2.4
Nicaragua	5.4	2.3
El Salvador	5.7	1.9
Paraguay	5.3	1.5
Bolivia	2.9	1
Guatemala	2.7	0.8
Non-weighted average	4.7	3.3
Weighted average	4.6	3.5
Total average	4.6	3

Latin America, it is also true that there has been no lack of sudden economic accelerations in the region. Along with Asia, Latin America had the greatest number of periods of accelerated growth during the second half of the twentieth century.

This macroeconomic volatility has had its counterpart in the political and institutional realms, since both reinforce each other as in a closed-circuit process. Argentina continues to have a particularly high rate of turnover in its government ministers, and this instability highlights (or sometimes reflects) the unexpected economic shocks it has been prone to over the last two decades, the last one being a major massive debt default and currency devaluation by the end of 2001. During the presidencies of Raúl Alfonsín (1983–1989) and of Carlos Menem (1989–1999) the cabinet instability was comparable. The average ministerial term in each administration was 2.5 months and 2.8 months, respectively. This instability later intensified under the governments of Fernando de la Rúa (1999–2001) and Eduardo Duhalde (2002–2003), with ministerial rotations every 0.8 and 0.9 month, respectively. In other words, since democracy was restored in 1983, Argentina has averaged a new minister of economics and finance every two months. Parliamentary terms also are characterized by instability and short temporal horizons. Elected officials in Argentina enjoy, on average, a single parliamentary mandate, whereas their counterparts in the U.S. Congress are elected to five to six terms. In fact, between 1983 and 2000 the reelection rate in Argentina was below 20 percent, in contrast to over 80 percent in the United States during the twentieth century and 60 percent in Chile after its return to democracy. Recent events in Argentina thus revive its history of political instability, but with an important nuance: it now takes place within a democratic framework. From the first coup d'état in 1930 until the end of the twentieth century, democratic government in Argentina suffered six interruptions. During the period 1930–2000, this instability effectively induced mandates of relatively brief duration: scarcely 2.6 years on average for presidents, 2.9 for parliamentary officials, and 1.9 for the provincial governors. These short terms inhibited the enactment of incremental economic policies. This instability also extended to all institutions. Argentina's Supreme Court, where the median duration of mandates between 1960 and 1990 barely reached 5 years, was not spared, in contrast to the United States during the same period (where Supreme Court judges have lifetime appointments and therefore are less sensitive to political fluctuations). The pattern in Argentina continues to be similar to the Latin American standards, since in Chile (in some respects the region's most advanced country in terms of both democracy and a market economy deepening) average terms exceed those of Argentina by scarcely a year. By the same token, the rotation rate for governors of Argentina's central bank was high; they changed approximately every 15 months after the return to democracy in 1983. Since the 1930s, when the institution was created, there have been

36 governors, with an average term of 2 years. For instance, after April 2002, when President Duhalde appointed Roberto Lavagna as Minister of Finance, the Banco Central de la República de Argentina saw a rapid succession of four different leaders: Mario Bléjer, Aldo Pignanelli, Alfonso Prat-Gay, and, finally, Martín Redrado, who was appointed in September 2004.

Comparing Argentina with Chile is instructive for gauging the variation in the Latin America's institutional trajectories. The Chilean Constitution of 1833 lasted nearly 100 years. The institution of the presidency has also been gradually solidified: after 1891, with the notable exception of Salvador Allende, all Chilean presidents have completed their elected terms. Despite the regime changes, and the coup that overthrew the democratically elected socialist president Salvador Allende, Chile's institutions were particularly stable. Since its inception in 1925, Chile's federal tax authority has had fourteen directors. Although two were at their posts less than a year, the remaining twelve averaged approximately 8 years in office.

Yet if we extend the comparison to all Latin American countries, we can see that with respect to the rotation of ministerial appointments Argentina turns out to be less exceptional. Over the 1990s, the three presidents of Costa Rica and those of Uruguay each went through an average of 18 cabinet ministers and 21 cabinet ministers respectively, in contrast to 40 ministers in the case of Colombia's presidents during the same decade. If we consider Menem's two terms and the interrupted one of De la Rúa—from then on volatility would become more extreme—with an average of 23 ministers per president, Argentina shows a relatively reasonable rate of ministerial wear and tear. As Peru's president between 1990 and 2000, Alberto Fujimori had a pronounced tendency to reorganize his cabinet frequently by juggling his ministers: during his three terms he had nearly 100 different ministers.

The decreases in tension that accompanied the financial crises in the 1990s illustrate this region's tendency to very real speculative fevers. While the frequency of financial and economic crises is higher in Latin America than in any other world region, during the 1990s the speed of recovery also appears to have accelerated. It took Mexico 7 years to recover from the 1982 debt crisis and to return to the international capital markets, but barely 7 months after the episode known as the 1994 Tequila Crisis, Mexico once again was issuing sovereign debt obligations. In terms of economic growth, though the Latin American GDP's recovery from the 1995 and 1999 crises was quicker than the recovery of 2002–03, it was less solid than the recovery after the crisis of 2003. (See figure 3.1.) In 2004, Latin America registered a growth rate close to 6 percent of GDP. For the first time in 40 years, all of Latin America's economies showed positive and synchronized rates of growth two consecutive years. This positive and synchronized growth was repeated in 2005. The economic historians Gerardo della

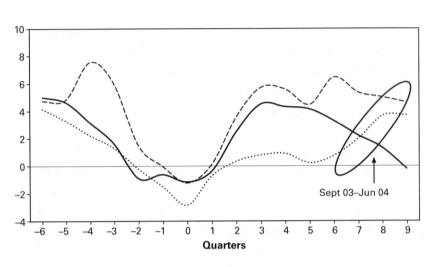

Figure 3.1
Latin American GDP performance since recessions (% annual growth).
---: 1995. —: 1999. ⋯: 2002–2003.

Paolera and Alan Taylor estimate that the ability to recover from financial crises accelerated during the course of the twentieth century: whereas the crises of 1913–14, 1929–1931, and 1980–81 each required 6 or 7 years for the region to return to previous growth levels, the 1988–1990 recovery took only 4 years and the 1994–95 recovery only 2 years.

Another prevailing but incorrect stereotype regarding Latin American countries is their solid reputation as serial defaulters that repeatedly fail to honor their debts. Yet long-term economic history reveals that over the past five centuries the record for government defaults belongs to a European country. Spain defaulted thirteen times between the sixteenth and twentieth centuries. Venezuela and Ecuador have nine defaults each. Together, France and Germany experienced eight defaults and were high on the list of serial defaulters.

Economic history also shows that it is possible to escape the debt trap, and in this regard Spain offers a remarkable example. During the twentieth century, Spain met all its debt obligations and modernized its economy with remarkable speed. In more recent years, its integration into the European Union has considerably reduced the risk premiums associated with its government obligations, and its economy has become less sensitive to the shocks of emerging countries. In this way, the differential between Spanish and German sovereign debt obligations—that is the Spanish risk premium—has diminished. When the Mexican crisis took place in 1994, the differential was more than 150 basis points between its 10-year bonds and German Treasury bills of the same duration. Several years later, when the Russian crisis occurred, it was only 50 basis points. During the 1999 Brazilian crisis, the deviation had been practically eliminated, with a differential of only 15 basis points. For the Latin American economies this is a lesson to remember, especially if we consider that this is a region where, during the twentieth century and especially in the two last decades, the majority of suspended debt payments were concentrated. Today, the world's four main serial defaulters are Ecuador, Venezuela, Liberia, and Turkey. The greatest default of recent history, in nominal value and in absolute value was Argentina's in 2001. (Argentina has defaulted five times.)

Chile appears to have assimilated the lesson. Having defaulted four times in its history, it drastically reduced its external debt. This outstanding debt surpassed 135 percent of its GDP in 1985, but decreased to approximately 30 percent by 2005. The reduction has been accomplished by resolutely following orthodox economic policies. The time when a country like Mexico could survive while failing to meet its debt and while defaulting regularly appears to be past. Mexico spent nearly 60 percent of the period 1825–1945, but less than 10 percent of the period since 1945, in default. Like Spain earlier, and like Chile in the past two decades, Mexico has managed to escape the debt trap.

The Waltzing Paradigms

Economic fashions proliferated abundantly in Latin America, as typified by the wave of neo-liberal policies that flooded the region during the 1990s. This wave lasted several years and affected nearly all the countries in the region, as did the previous structuralist and Marxist waves. The UN's Economic Commission for Latin America and the Caribbean (ECLAC) produced the famous industrial theories favoring import substitution promoted by Raúl Prebisch. This economist, born in Argentina, became one of ECLAC's most influential leaders. He is known for his contribution to structuralist

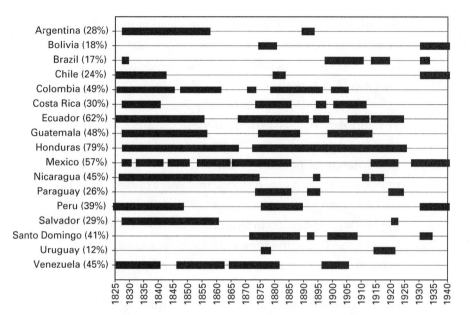

Figure 3.2
Periods during which various countries were in default of payment,
1825–1945. Source: Michael Tomz, Stanford University.

economics—particularly the Prebisch-Singer hypothesis,
which was the basis of the Dependency Theory that
spread all over Latin America during the 1950s and the
1960s. The last and most recent economic policy wave
was hidden in a deeper sea, and is manifested today in
the hangover from the receding neo-liberal wave, a point
that should be emphasized here.

Many of the initiatives that have characterized the politics of liberalization and privatization since the 1990s
were started in the wake of a crisis or a deteriorating

economic situation. Difficulties often lead to the initiation
of reforms that entail social costs. These costs are perceived by leaders as being the lesser evil with respect to
the projected benefits or to the cost of doing nothing. For
example, since 1974 when Chile pioneered privatization
in Latin America, Argentina undertook a bold program
15 years later in what was practically the world's first
deregulation of postal services. In Mexico the number of
public enterprises was reduced in a short period by a factor of 5, going from more than 1,000 at the beginning of
the 1980s to under 200 in less then a decade. By the beginning of the 1990s, the region as a whole accounted for 35
percent of all privatization schemes being undertaken
throughout the world, making Latin America one of the
places where privatizations occurred most quickly and
deeply. The intensity and the speed of these Latin
American asset transfers to the private sector amounted
to more than half of the benefits derived from privatization by all emerging markets during the first half of the
1990s.

Similarly, with regard to the opening of commerce and
free trade, Latin America has moved at a sustained pace,
as indicated by the proliferation of bilateral and multilateral trade agreements. Without a doubt, one of the most
remarkable is that of Mercosur, a regional trade agreement signed in Asunción, Paraguay in 1991 by four
countries of the Southern Cone (Argentina, Brazil,
Uruguay, and Paraguay) and which became effective
January 1, 1995. Mexico offers an even more significant

example. In spite of a strong protectionist and nationalist tradition, this country signed the North American Free Trade Agreement (NAFTA) with the United States and Canada, which came into effect on January 1, 1994. NAFTA pointed to a change in scope. A self-centered strategy following an outdated paradigm based on import substitution was succeeded by a particularly dynamic strategy of opening to commercial trade and entering into global exchange. Mexico, one of the signatories to the General Agreement on Trade and Tariffs (GATT) in 1986, became the only Latin American state to conclude an agreement of this type with the United States and Canada, and also the only one that is a founding member of the European Bank for Reconstruction and Development (EBRD). In May 1994, Mexico became a member of the selective Organisation for Economic Cooperation and Development. Today, nearly every Latin American country hopes to achieve a free-trade agreement with the United States, even if it is only a minimal one, and Chile, Mexico's imitator in this instance, has been knocking on the door of the OECD. The rush toward free-trade agreements with the United States has been intensified since 2000 and is exemplified by the U.S. Congress' passage, in July 2005, of the Central America Free Trade Agreement, which links all the Central American countries and the Dominican Republic with the United States. With the exception of Venezuela, all the Andean countries have engaged in an intensive trade flirtation with the U.S.

These economic policies have been spearheaded by a generation of leaders, sometimes precipitately referred to as technocrats. Menem and Cavallo in Argentina, Salinas and Zedillo in Mexico, and in Chile the Chicago Boys and then Aylwin and Frei—these leaders have in common a high incidence of academic education abroad. Mexico's Pedro Aspe (educated at MIT) and Chile's Alejandro Foxley (educated at Wisconsin), each of whom became his country's minister of economics and finance, illustrate the generational shift to people who share a worldview and who equally value the free market and liberal democracy.

The most surprising aspect of the "great transformation" in Latin America, however, is the persistence of personalities who resemble characters in a novel more than they resemble technocrats. In fact, the speed, the breadth, and the depth of the experimental transformations in numerous economies in the region would not have been possible without the extraordinary conjunction of a series of factors owing as much to rapidly deteriorating economic situations—which demanded a change of direction—as to the appearance of a skilled team of economic advisors that benefited from a singular political umbrella upheld by populist chameleons, interventionist the day before the elections, who turned into free-market neo-liberals the night they entered the presidential palace.

But these personalities did inhabit the end of the twentieth century and the beginning of the new millennium in

Latin America. Many of them have implemented an extraordinary shift in policy, enabling their countries to tolerate the shock treatments imposed by the neo-liberal medicine. Without a doubt, the archetype of the Latin American chameleon was Carlos Menem, who enacted the entire populist repertoire of the Latin gaucho, and at the same time committed his country to one of the region's speediest economic transformations by dancing to a furious neo-liberal tango. In this way, it seems that the nostalgic habits of authoritarianism, populism, clientelism (systems based on patronage), and those of the revolutionary armed forces have blended but still retain the phraseology of yesterday. Should we take this to mean that the conversion to the delights of Democracy and the Market is nothing more than a new facade destined to fool foreign investors with the camouflage of the Good Neo-Liberal?

Undoubtedly, the conversion to Democracy and to the Market at times acquires the traits of a paradigm shift. Certain intellectual trajectories in the region show to what extent adhering to these new values can be attributed to opportunistic calculations. But the paradox is only apparent, because what is playing out in Latin America today is not so much the emergence of a new paradigm, which would be applicable in all its conceptual rigidity, but the emergence of an economic model that is more concerned with the ethics of consequences than with the ethics of convictions. The priority given to the great theories effectively seems to be vanishing, as is

demonstrated by the shift in thought of the great multilateral agencies—not only the World Bank, but also the
ECLAC, the Corporación Andina de Fomento, and the
Inter-American Development Bank (which have more
influence in Latin America). The region is thus benefiting
from more realistic economic policies, more attuned to
practical efficiency than to ideological integrity.

In fact, contrary to the paradox previously outlined,
the shift in emphasis to the Market and to Democracy
invalidates the idea of a simple permutation of paradigms. The conversions of many intellectuals, economists and politicians, were broad and deeply profound,
nourished by disappointments and disenchantment with
revolutions. Besides the disillusionment in revolutionary
platforms, Latin America's real historical experiences of
authoritarian government contributed to its reevaluation
of Democracy and the Market. In this sense, beyond the
strategic conversions that obey a simple dialectic of interests, the frequency of ideological conversions, assumed
politically or intellectually, has often led to profound and
painful self-examinations.

These conversions were occasionally premature, as in
the case of Hernán Büchi, a noteworthy minister under
Augusto Pinochet who was in charge of Chile's finances
between 1985 and 1989, who was rumored to have had
youthful affinities with the Movimiento de la Izquierda
Revolucionaria (Movement of the Revolutionary Left).
Very quickly after his return from Columbia University,

Büchi turned to the free-market liberals of the Chicago School who had then begun to associate themselves with Chile's military regime. Conversions were often progressive, nurtured by historical facts or pulled forward by intellectual encounters, by proofs and doubts, as shown by the intellectual trajectory of Carlos Ominami, the economic minister under Patricio Aylwin, Chile's first democratically elected president after Pinochet's military dictatorship ended. Like Büchi, Ominami had roots in the MIR, but had a political rebirth making him receptive to the virtues of the Market and Democracy as a result of the 1973 coup d'état. The conversion of the Peruvian writer and intellectual Mario Vargas Llosa, who for a long time was closely connected to various movements on the Latin American revolutionary left, took place over a period that spanned from 1970, the year in which the Cuban poet Heberto Padilla was incarcerated to 1980, when he discovered the ideas of the liberal philosopher Karl Popper. Vargas Llosa became a strong proponent of these ideas and a strong force in the diffusion of Karl Popper's thought throughout the region.

The study of these transformations throughout Latin America has yet to begin. Many authors have underscored the importance of the international factor, the global time of market democracy, which was put into ample practice and helped transform Latin America's frames of reference. But beyond these exogenous factors, whether international or national, it is possible to under-

stand these altered preferences not as linear learning
processes affected by the successive shocks of global or
national history, but rather as individual trajectories subject to the beneficial factors of convergence. For many of
Latin America's intellectual and political elites,
Democracy and the Market have been integrated or rein-
tegrated into their political and economic alphabet and
into their expectational horizons after a long process of
disillusionment and disenchantment with ideologies.
Similarly, for many members of Chile's Christian
Democratic Party and for Mexico's reformers, for example, the Market was gradually integrated within their
framework. This shift was because their observations
and experiences indicated that in order to guarantee
growth, it was necessary to have the Market take priority over centralized planning. Allegiance to the Market
stemmed from empirical observations as much as it did
from theoretical convictions. This idea of a horizon of
expectations helps us to understand what has been at the
heart of political democratizations and economic liberalizations: learning, discovery, even creation and acquisi-
tion on the part of the agents involved, new cognitive
maps, and, most importantly, new ways to craft political
economy.

From Utopianism to Possibilism

The great Latin American transformation at the end of
the twentieth century is not the arrival of the Good Neo-

Liberal. There has not been, as one might think, a shift from one paradigm to another but rather, the emergence of a new cognitive style. In other words, this attests to the failure of the very idea of a political utopia and of the political economy of the impossible, the failure of a cognitive style that, like macroeconomic populism or monetarism, turned out to consist of defenses and supplemental illustrations of the same utopian failures.

In fact, we are witnessing the emergence of the politics of the possible— humbler, less oriented toward the indefinite future and more toward the present, and more concerned with effective outcomes than with conceptual purity. This emergence marks in particular the failure of convictions rooted in the belief in salutary individual sacrifices at the altar of great historical ideals. As the British philosopher Isaiah Berlin wrote, the failure of the idea that "thinkers from Bacon to the present have been inspired by the certainty that there must exist a total solution: that in the fullness of time, whether by the will of God or by human effort, the reign of irrationality, injustice and misery will end; man will be liberated, and will no longer by the plaything of forces beyond his control."[1]

At the heart of the process of political democratization and economic liberalization in Latin America exists the implicit or explicit recognition of the need for reconciling conflicting interests and values. This involves the idea that realizing some ideals means achieving other ones will be impossible. For example, the idea of pursuing justice for those who were persecuted by dictatorships may represent a real risk of losing advances already gained toward democracy, and that neither liberal shock therapies nor the developmentalist medicines will usher in the nirvana of economic development.

The emergence of possibilism stands out among a diverse renewal of socialist currents, in Chile and Brazil, for instance, which are now more flexible and more moderate than was true in the past. In Chile and outside the country for the one that became political refugees in Western and Eastern Europe, some socialist revivals embarked upon a broad program of political renovation, reevaluating formal democracy by abandoning an instrumental conception of it in favor of reconsidering anew the laws of the market, without ignoring its limitations. This is not specific to the Latin American left, nor is it complete. It partly subscribes to the procedural framework of political democratization and economic liberalization, in the course of which a new understanding and art of the possible has been achieved, that is, it is a result of a dynamic series of adjustments and readjustments of preferences.

The Temporalization of the Market Economy

The transformation of these reference frames has been accompanied by an adjustment of temporal horizons. We have seen this as democracy emerges in the region: its arrival has been accompanied by a spectacular return to concentrating on the present and a corresponding devaluation of utopianism's elusive time horizons. In the economic sphere, we have witnessed an accompanying focus on the present, as shorter time horizons emerge, also characteristic of the market economy. The shift from one reference frame dominated by the Revolution and the State to another dominated by Democracy and the Market lends credibility to this temporal shift, the first involving long-term planning horizons, and the second shorter ones.

As we have seen, the advent of Democracy marks a tightening of temporal horizons, a focus on the present to the detriment of resplendent futures. It is a matter of political temporality very different from that of the Revolution, dominated by a horizon of millenarian possibilities. The State has its own time frame, different from the market's, and since the fifteenth century the time of the modern nation-state has been imposed on religious time, affirming possibilism over prophetism. Bernouilli's discovery, in the sixteenth century, of how to calculate probabilities and statistics reinforced the credibility of political forecasts and economic foresight. In the late nineteenth century, the development of time zones and the standardization of time allowed the coordination of train travel and the organization of production during the industrial age, much like the nation-state rendered the concept of time secular and linked it to political machinations and engineering. Over the course of the twentieth century, the State developed instruments to control production systems, panels, and social indicators

meant to guarantee the present and the future of its
citizens: to protect them from the vicissitudes of
Providence, increase their welfare, and, most important,
their hope for their lives. For several decades the dominant timeframe was long-term since State-centered
regimes and socialist regimes both aspire, though in different ways, to last a long time.

In the last two decades of the twentieth century, a
much more powerful time horizon emerged, linked to
capitalism and to the market economy. The perspective
of real time and the imperative of speed, the race to
achievement and efficiency, were accompanied by a flattening of temporal horizons that forced states to adapt
their reactions to the speed and timing of financial markets, the new masters of the clock. Two time-based logics
confronted each other: on the one hand, that of the State,
meant to ensure stability and longevity, and on the other,
that of the markets, which hungered for speed and for
short-term gain. The ascendancy of the financial sphere,
tied to the short term and to speed, was the last impetus
for capitalism to turn to short time horizons and to focus
on real time. Whereas in 1960 the term of ownership for
Latin American equity stocks averaged about 7 years, it
was only 7 months by the end of the twentieth century. In
financial markets, buying and selling orders can be exe-
cuted extremely rapidly. In the same way, while in the
middle of the twentieth century the publication of annual company reports in March of the following year
seemed like an unparalleled feat, today many American

companies close their annual books in the first weeks of the following fiscal year, which is three times faster than the 90-day term permitted by the financial authorities. The standardization of accounting practices and the takeover of the real economy by the financial regulators pushed companies around the world to follow this kind of quarterly financial "strip tease," which they must submit to in order to participate in the international "beauty contest" and to stoke the desire of the international investment community.

During the twentieth century Latin America did not remain in the wings while the market's temporal laws were compressed. In the realm of economics, the flattening of time horizons into the immediate present illustrated a structural adjustment which was, above all, a temporal adjustment. An economic structure that sought stable horizons in which to deploy strategies involving industrialization and import substitution was succeeded by a much more open economy in which global time has also accelerated. The economic history of the last decade is, in fact, nothing but the complete adjustment of the entire Latin American continent to this accelerated global time, now dominated by the short temporal horizons of the market economy. From this perspective, liberalization processes, regulation, and privatization can be interpreted as the temporalization of the economy. To privatize is also to privilege the immediacy of quick financial gains, to emphasize short-term profits, and to diminish the State's capacity to control the workings of the economy, to plan a country's economic future by implementing industrial strategies and imposing regulations upon various sectors.

One of the outstanding examples of this temporalization on the Latin American economy has been the privatization of pension plans. Chile pioneered this practice at the beginning of the 1980s, and pension privatization was adopted by the majority of the region's countries in the 1990s. These reforms transfer the task of ensuring the future from the public sphere to the private sector. In other words, the State transferred its capacity to ensure the future of its citizens to the Market. The certainty, guaranteed by the State, of enjoying a given level of financial security once the age of retirement was reached, was transferred to the market economy. Afterwards, it was mainly the Market (albeit with the State, in the shadows, in charge of careful regulation of this sector), with its rises and falls, that guaranteed future incomes and the pensions of the retired. Thus the State yielded its capacity to ensure the future to the new "master of the clocks," that is to say, the Market. As long as the stock market went up, as was the case in Chile until 1995 (annual gains of 12 percent for retirement funds), the survival of pensions was assured. The market, time's new master, and in particular the future, seemed unassailable. When, however, losses accumulated (in 1995 retirement funds grew an average of 2 percent), the brakes were engaged: the other owner of the clocks, the State, once again had to intervene with its arsenal of regulations and adjustments.

It is a paradox that term "globalization" hides a purely spatial metaphor. If we understand this much-used
term to mean the market economy's triumph, perhaps
above all globalization denotes a temporal reality. In this
sense, it could be understood as the compacting of time
and space. Global transportation costs from one point to
another have been reduced considerably, from the financial viewpoint as well as from the temporal point of view.
The reduction of these costs, thanks to infrastructure
improvements in roads, railways, ports, and airports, has
become a strategic asset in the global competitiveness
race. Customs procedures are bottlenecks that sometimes
result in significant time delays: in Estonia, for example,
customs formalities for imports are resolved in 48 hours,
while in Ecuador these can last up to sixteen days,
according to the World Bank's "investment climate"
studies.

The weakness of Latin America's transportation infrastructure constitutes an obstacle to its entry into the global economy, for which the cost and speed of transporting
merchandise remain a decisive comparative advantage.
The terms and the waiting times associated with crossing
borders and completing various customs forms—additional dead time from the economic viewpoint—can be
prolonged to five days in the axis of Rio de Janeiro-
Valparaíso or even São Paulo-Buenos Aires. In Central
America, the terms and waiting time for imports and
exports to pass through customs may constitute up to 40
percent of the duration of commercial shipment. With

regard to maritime transport, the terms established in
Latin America, calculated in business days, are twice as
long as those in the United States. With the exception of
Chile (three days) and Mexico (five days), whose ports of
entry have customs regulations and procedures similar
to those of the developed countries, the remaining Latin
American countries have build-ups resulting in lost time
and efficiency, downtime that if eliminated would accelerate exports, both within and outside the region.

The potential gains related to reducing transportation
costs are relatively important to Latin American countries. Privatization and competition policies enforced by
some countries have certainly allowed for significant
improvements in these services. With regard to ports, for
instance, the waiting times for containers in Colombia
have been reduced from approximately 10 days to a few
hours due to privatizing port operations. But considerable time differentials remain in comparison to other
countries like China, for instance, which is increasingly
important in world trade. With regard to port infrastructures (which account to nearly 80 percent of the total
trade of the developed countries), Hong-Kong has one of
the world's most efficient ports. Substantial improvements to the port infrastructures in Latin American countries like Mexico, for example, will allow it to respond to
the competitive challenges posed by China, since Mexico
enjoys a significant strategic advantage: its geographic
proximity to the United States, the largest and most
dynamic market in the world. Transporting a product

from Mexico to the United States takes on average 6 days, while it requires 24 days to ship from China to the United States. The costs play out in favor of Mexico. This spatial and temporal advantage, as underscored by economic geography, is far from being marginal in terms of costs: for each additional day of sea-going transport shipment, the probability that American companies will choose to import from China is reduced by 1 percent.

In the real economy, global time horizons are dominated by the frantic search for profit and productivity, which demand a careful handling of fulfillment terms and delivery methods, and of the inventory management necessary to avoid unproductive warehousing. Under these new time pressures, businesses limit their strategies to the planning horizon delimited by their annual reports— or rather, their quarterly performance as measured every three months—while product life cycles are shortened by the same measure. Time management becomes the strategic asset par excellence, and given the ever-quicker obsolescence of products, the speed of market penetration is an important factor in success or failure.

The labor market also supports these time constraints. The concept of lifetime employment has been relegated to a relic from the past in the museum of old-time capitalism, as today employment periods are shorter-term or even temporary.

The most complete expression of the modern economic temporalities undoubtedly is found in the realm of finance. In the financial world, real time has given way to even-more-immediate time frames, consisting of accelerations and anticipations, as future anticipations compress the temporal margins of the present. The most common characteristic of financial markets is that they effectively discount even the lengthiest expectations of the future and undo the synchronizations of the present. One of the paradoxes of the financial world is the ability to answer the question posed by the physicist Stephen Hawking, who, in the preface to *A Brief History of Time*, asks why we remember the past but not the future. In many ways, the financial markets remember the future. Thanks to the game of anticipation and intertemporal arbitrage, financial markets have the ability to transform the conjectures about the future into a relevant event within the immediate present, improbable future prognoses into tangible and immediate news. This is how in the world of finance temporal horizons go against the immediate present.

Far from the arduous adjustment processes in real economies, financial market expectations can be enacted immediately through the reconstruction of portfolios channeled through the Bloomberg monitors. On a tiny space of a few square inches, entire panels of real economies, countries and businesses are caught in the trap of (sometimes irrational) financial exuberance. The impatience of traders and portfolio managers, based on a potential future event anticipated by some months or years, is transferred directly to the immediate present where their calculations have real impact. This frenetic

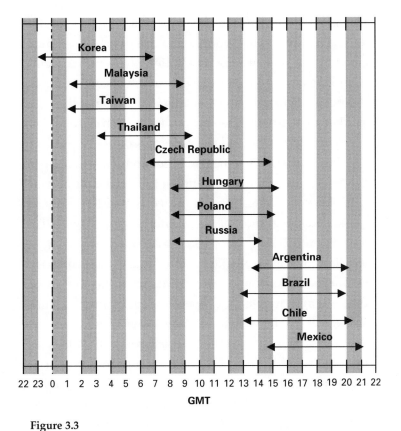

Figure 3.3
Time zones and schedules of emerging markets. (GMT: Greenwich Mean Time.)

moment-by-moment activity is also permanent, since the sun never sets on the world's financial markets. As indicated by the play of time zone differentials, for emerging economies as well as for markets in advanced countries, financial arbitrage never ceases. With some financial market always open, the dance of figures, charts and data is never interrupted and the present is omnipresent.

Latin America's emerging economies must steer though this unstable international financial environment consisting of short temporal horizons, sudden accelerations, and the pursuit of speed and revised tempos. The instruments these countries use to navigate in these treacherous waters are often rudimentary: their compasses are macroeconomic instruments, monetary or fiscal, that attempt to separate operating risks from drifting shipwrecks. The structural adjustments which Latin American countries were subjected to in the 1900s are thus inscribed in the accelerated time frames of market economies and financial markets. In general, privatizations took place at full speed in order to allow governments to fatten their coffers without enduring the slow, unpopular, and painful transformation of their fiscal systems. For businesses, and particularly foreign businesses swooping down on the gold to be found in Latin America's El Dorado, privatizations turned into additional opportunities to acquire important market shares quickly by skipping the slow and difficult process of creating a new enterprise from scratch, especially in countries where the business conditions are complex and of such nature that these concerns can cancel out the competitive advantage of speed.

In order to adapt to the temporal laws of the market economy, Latin American leaders adopted and adapted broad reforms, some introduced gradually, some enacted at an accelerated pace. The relative speed of their implementation constitutes, at any rate, one of the principal characteristics of the Latin American reform processes, which give priority to "shock therapies" over a more gradual policy reform and piecemeal engineering. In 90 percent of cases of the privatization processes, the choice was for quick asset transfers. Between 1990 and 1995, more than 700 businesses were transferred from the visible hand of the State to the invisible hand of the market. Regarding inflation stabilization, 70 percent of the 24 countries studied implemented urgent shock therapies. This speed in some areas contrasts with more incremental policies in other realms. According to the estimates and studies of the Inter-American Development Bank Research Department, at the peak of the mid-1990s reform cycle, rapid liberalization was advocated in only 50 percent of the cases concerning trade liberalization, and in fiscal matters scarcely 25 percent of new policies were enacted quickly.

Throughout Latin America, economic deregulations intended to reduce commercial trade barriers and to compress downtimes, both regarded as lags that facilitate corruption and foster comparative economic disadvantages, have flourished. The margins for maneuvering are important, with broad inequalities between advanced economies and emerging ones. The time required for establishing a business in the developed economies is relatively short compared with the especially prolonged terms found in emerging economies. In *The Other Path* the Peruvian economist Hernando de Soto calculated that in 1983 the time required to complete the bureaucratic requirements to start a business enterprise in Peru took 298 days. Twenty years later, after the structural adjustments of the liberal years, the time differential was greatly reduced: incorporating a business in Peru now took 100 days, a reduction of two-thirds. Yet Peru's road ahead remains considerable if we compare this result to Australia, New Zealand, and Canada, the champions of temporal adjustment (terms of 2 or 3 days) or to Chile and Panama, the Latin American champions of brief terms and low transaction costs (19 days and 28 days, respectively), or even with European countries (among them France, which has terms approaching 53 days). It should be mentioned that Peru, having reduced terms to approximately 100 days, is ahead of Spain, which has terms that extend to 115 days.

On average, the 13.5 bureaucratic steps necessary to incorporate a new business in Latin America during 2000 was higher than in any other economy, that taken together average 9.6 steps. The terms to complete these requirements were also longer (93 days on average in Latin America, compared to 58 outside the region). Studies by the World Bank show that Latin America made spectacular progress between 2000 and 2004: practically all countries in the region reduced the time needed for starting a new business. In Brazil, Mexico, and Chile, the time has been shortened by over 50 percent. Uruguay holds the record in this regard, with a reduction of 70 percent.

Time savings are also reflected in the legal realm through reducing terms and amount of transactions. Foreign direct investors participate in the race for speed. In the electrical utilities sector, for instance, the quest for reduced downtime and waiting times for connection became systematic. In the telecommunications sector, too, the new entrants, most of them foreigners like the Spanish-based company Telefónica or its Italian rival Telecom Italia, attempted to reduce the waiting time necessary for installing telephone lines. In São Paulo, for example, Telefónica reduced waits for these lines from 40 months to 5 months between 1977 and 2001. In Argentina, those waiting periods were reduced from 49 months (a record of slowness) in 1994 to 1 month in 2001. This temporal adjustment is particularly impressive in Peru, where waiting periods for telephone line installations extended to 6 years in 1994, an eternity compared with the 3 months needed by the beginning of the 2000s. In Mexico, the waiting time for new telephone lines went from nearly 900 days to fewer than 30. But there still remain important pockets of delay. More than eleven transactions are needed to start a new business in Latin America; that is, two more than in the countries of Southeast Asia. The waiting periods are also longer, 70

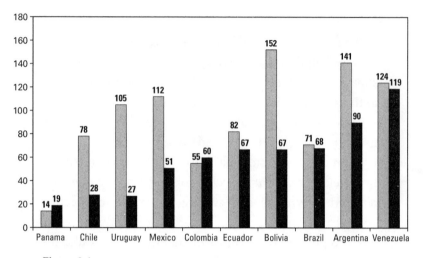

Figure 3.4
Number of days required to incorporate a business in 2000 (gray bars) and in 2004 (black bars). Based on data from World Bank, World Economic Forum, and Harvard University.

days on average in Latin America in 2004, compared to only 46 days in Southeast Asia. We should also mention the time constraints that inhibit the circulation of merchandise. In the race against the clock which competition demands, it appears that the dynamics of regional integration act as catalysts for change. In 2005 the World Bank found that 60 percent of the reforms designed to reduce the bureaucratic waiting times and to accelerate business creation were enacted within the European Union (one-third of the countries in Europe are members of the EU). Colombia, which began negotiating a free-trade agreement with the United States in 2005, is the only Latin American country among the world's ten principal reformers. In total, the new data from the 2005 study confirm that the race against the clock has intensified: 58 of the 145 countries that figure in the World Bank Report titled *Doing Business* have simplified their bureaucratic requirement and reinforced property rights since the previous year.

As in the matter of telephone line installations, there is still a disparity, underlined by studies done by the World Bank, in Latin America's investment climate. Businesses claim that, on average, the waiting times they face for the connection of telephone lines are similar in Brazil (18 days) and in China (15 days). These waiting periods are much longer in other countries such as Honduras, where they can take up to 140 days. In the competitive race for speed, these distances are clearly maintained and are considerable between one country and another, but also within a country itself. There are notable differences between Shanghai, where it takes 13 days to obtain a new telephone line, and Peking, where 21 are needed. Similarly, in Brazil the differences among regions are important, and some fit better than others with global temporalities.

This time adjustment can be read in light of macroeconomic variables. One of the most spectacular and positive Latin American transformations has taken place in monetary policy. During the 1980s, inflation in some countries reached new heights: nearly 600 percent in Brazil on average, 800 percent in Argentina, 1,200 percent

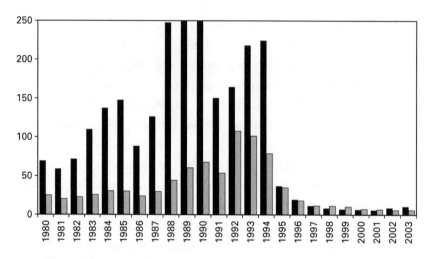

Figure 3.5
Inflation rates (in %) as barometers of preference for the present in
Latin America (black bars) and in all developed countries (gray bars).
Source: BBVA 2005.

in Peru, and more than 5,000 percent in Nicaragua. In
barely a few years, however, hyperinflation was stopped
and inflation rates were stabilized in a lasting way. As of
2000, these rates reached a level below 10 percent for the
region as a whole.

This convergence toward low rates of inflation is
important, since inflation is a true indicator of preferences in a given society. When inflation rates are high,
time horizons narrow, States become incapable of planning for the future, businesses become incapable of pro-
ducing according to the laws of supply and demand, and
households are unable to save, since monetary erosion

compresses all future time horizons into a single present. From this angle, the 1980s, during which Latin America was marked by hyperinflation, was a decade that can be characterized as focusing on the present. By controlling inflation, the States gained a vision of the future, businesses were able to adjust their prices and their output efficiently, and households were able to consume and to save in the absence of constantly skyrocketing prices. In this sense, the 1990s were years of reconstruction (albeit limited) of a more stable and less utopian temporal horizon.

In spite of the economic progress that accompanied these reform efforts, the margins for maneuvering continued to be wide. It is true that Latin America has committed itself to a broad agenda for reform. For some countries, however, reforms continue to be incomplete, and some have turned out to be disappointing. Dissatisfaction is prevalent in the entire region. According to the annual polls of Latinobarómetro, since 1997, the number of people who believe that the economic situation is bad has increased in fourteen of the seventeen countries analyzed. Additionally, while earlier privatization was judged positively, a significant majority of Latin Americans now perceive privatization as not being beneficial. Only one-fourth of Latin Americans currently believe that privatizations have been positive for their countries, whereas nearly half of Latin Americans supported these reforms in 1996.

This dissatisfaction is directly linked to sparse economic growth. The negative sentiments among Latin

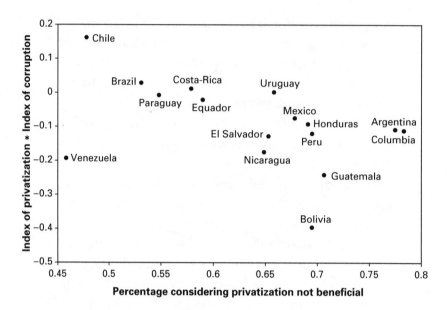

Figure 3.6
Corruption and opposition to privatization in Latin America. Source:
Lora and Panizza 2003.

Americans indicate disenchantment with previous
reforms often sold as definitive panaceas for the region's
ills and the shortcomings of the privatization processes
results from institutional weaknesses and its corollary:
high rates of corruption. In fact, as figure 3.6 shows, there
is an important correlation between opposing privatization and the incidence of corruption. In Chile, where privatization was intense and took place in an institutional
and ethical environment with a low risk of corruption,
support for these reforms eroded much less.

The negative perception of privatization harkens back to institutional deficiencies. Entire countries are convinced that even in a hypothetical case where they would benefit from the process, the advantages accruing to the political and economic elites would be considerably greater. Numerous studies highlight the fact that privatizing water, telecommunications and electric services in Argentina, Bolivia, Nicaragua, and Mexico have been positive for consumers. In spite of frequent price increases, access to these services improved substantially and has been extended to disadvantaged populations. Among them, use of these services has increased rather than declined in the wake of reforms, as is the case of Brazil, Colombia, and Peru. When privatization was accompanied by large restructuring and broad staff reductions, a significant number of people were able to recover their jobs over the next 5 years (45–50 percent in Argentina, 80–90 percent in Mexico). But the effects went beyond pure mercantile logic. In Argentina, for example, privatizing the delivery of water services was accompanied by a 5–10 percent reduction in the rate of infant mortality.

The studies undertaken by the economists from ECLAC and the Inter-American Development Bank show that reforms, although modest and sometimes (very) imperfect, had a positive effect despite the fact that poverty indicators have not improved. The effect of privatizations was revised downward at the beginning of 2000, especially in social matters. The first estimates

expected a positive effect on short-term growth and pre-
dicted a 2 percent improvement. The more recently
revised estimates show annual growth of less than 1 percent during the 1990s. The much-awaited acceleration of
growth did not take place. In some countries this effort
ended in dramatic macroeconomic accidents, as was the
case in Argentina in the early 2000s. In fact, on average,
the region's growth in per-capita GDP was relatively
modest in spite of the momentum from reforms—it barely reached 1.5 percent in the 1990s. This result, although
it exceeds the –0.6 percent of the 1980s, continues to be
inferior to the Southeast Asian champions, and Latin
American countries have not been able to reverse the
process of falling being developed countries in growth in
per-capita GDP.

Academic debates over the benefits and the limits of
these reforms have intensified. No doubt the first wave of
reforms erred on the side of optimism and credulity with
respect to these elaborate economic recipes prepared far
away from the sleepiness of extreme tropical poverty.
The good news is that the time of the prophets seems to
have been left behind. The millennial atmosphere has
given way to subtler tones: now, there is a turning away
from advocates of the Market and the State in their pure
unadulterated forms. The State is no longer seen as the
miracle worker many economists proclaimed it to be, nor
is the Market regarded as the divine institution that the
apostles of the Chicago School claimed it was. The insis-
tence on the shortcomings of the Market, of institutions,

and even the drastic economic interventions by governments is further evidence of the same movement of great
ideological tides. The bedrock of Latin America's reform
movement seems to have given way to something much
more promising, eclectic, and fertile.

In fact, contrary to excessively pessimistic views of the
region, though Latin Americans rate the process of privatization negatively, they do not confuse the benefits of the
market economy with its defects. In 2003, nearly two-
thirds of Latin Americans still believed that the market
economy and democracy were the best possible paths to
economic and political development. The results of the
2004 polls confirm this tendency. One of the most
remarkable results is the affirmation that the market
economy continues to be regarded by most Latin
Americans as the economic system that can best contribute to the development of countries. In Mexico, in
Brazil, in Colombia, in Peru, and even in Venezuela,
60–70 percent favor the market system, and this percentage exceeds 50 percent in every country.

Latin America's lingering malaise with regard to the
liberal reforms of the 1990s is certainly real. This can be
seen in the blocking of privatization in a number of
Andean countries, in the anti-globalization protests of
Evo Morales and his followers in Bolivia, and in the election of leaders who do not share the neo-liberal agenda of
their predecessors, such as Hugo Chávez in Venezuela,
Néstor Kirchner in Argentina, and Lucio Gutiérrez in
Ecuador.[2] Even so, the fantasy of a Latin America newly

obsessed with its authoritarian demons, whether populist or interventionist, turns out to be an exaggerated
reading of the region. Latin America can no longer be
seen as a land of crystal-clear waters and grand definitive
solutions. Rather, it offers a landscape of muddled
waters, where the dividing lines between statism and liberalism and between utopianism and pragmatism are
confused, but where the leaders no longer have carte
blanche to try out their medications and therapies on the
social body, where macroeconomic prudence now
trumps any fiscal or monetary adventure.

The time of great hopes is past, and with it the democratic enchantments and the great reforms of structural
adjustments. It also seems that we should not despair at
the death of the great reforming impulses. Evidence for
this bias for hope can be found in a careful study, directed by a team of Harvard economists headed by Ricardo
Hausmann and Dani Rodrik, of 83 episodes of sustained
growth (growth exceeding 2 percent during a period of at
least eight consecutive years) between 1957 and 1992. It
shows that the majority of these economic accelerations
were not preceded by big reforms or by great political or
economic ruptures. Although reforms were necessary to
maintain the rate of growth, an initial megalomania
seems an inadequate foundation on which to establish
sustained growth.

More pragmatic, less reliant on paradigms, more modest in their agendas for reform, and detached from the
illusions of yesterday, Latin American leaders are now

moving forward. From Chile to Brazil, including Mexico (but also Colombia, Costa Rica, and Uruguay), "possibilist" trajectories are being invented in which, as in all murky waters, pragmatic flows meet and mix, while the prevailing currents of the Good Neo-Liberals and the Good Revolutionaries fade away.

4   The Chilean Trajectory: From Liberalism to Possibilism

Chile is often presented as the Good Free-Marketeer poster child, the culmination of Latin America's neo-liberal economic trajectory. Over the last quarter-century, the Chilean economy has gone through a sweeping transformation driven by the government's unwavering commitment to market liberalization, transparency, and fiscal accountability. Rewarded by success, today this country is adorned with all the economic virtues and all the neo-liberal halos, a paragon of radical, free-market economic reform and a Latin paradise for investors. Yet this reading is simplistic, since the great lesson taken from Chile has not been the blind adoption of a single and absolute paradigm, but rather achieving an increasing distance from ideological fevers of all kinds. Above all, what stands out in the experience of the last three decades is Chile's pragmatic search for growth with equity, along a path increasingly free of rigid models either structural, Marxist, or neo-liberal.

Throughout the 1980s, the attitude of Chile's leaders and its opposing political groups became increasingly pragmatic. In particular, the Chilean leaders of the opposition understood that remaining attached to the pure ethics of conviction would increase the risk of remaining stuck in Pinochet's non-democratic regime and would continue living in a nation of enemies, under the military rule of a regime politically dictatorial and economically neo-liberal. During the 1960s and the 1970s radicalism was in fashion. Chile was transformed into a veritable laboratory where, paradigm after paradigm, economic policies consisted of an endless display of futures, an infinite succession of ruptures, without the possibility of incremental adjustments and readjustments. Whether the political economy of Eduardo Frei's "revolution in liberty" in the 1960s or Allende's "socialist revolution" or the Chicago Boys' "neo-liberal revolution" in the 1970s, all these theories had strong teleological dimensions and were configured according to a single revolutionary and utopian matrix.

The great landmark in Chile's contemporary history was not 1973, the year of the coup d'état, but rather the Latin American debt crisis and the ensuing Chilean banking crisis, which both took place at the beginning of the 1980s. After that critical juncture, and pressed by one of the most severe economic crises in Chilean as well as Latin American history, a more pragmatic focus on political economy emerged. The great news that comes to us from Chile is precisely one of liberation: Chile's leaders, whether on the left or on the right, no longer trust rigid economic paradigms of whatever stripe or hue.

Ending the Political Economy of the Impossible

The economic policies evoked by phrases such as the "ideology of sacrifice" and "the moment of global planning," whether structuralist, socialist, or monetarist, all share the same affinities with a utopian model that has broken with the old economic and political order. Yet these economic policies also tend to be rather projective, postponing the economic nirvana toward a distant promised land whose future path was made visible in turn by Marxism, and even neo-liberalism. In describing the period between the 1960s and the 1980s, the Chilean historian Mario Góngora wrote that "the tendency of the spirit of the times was to have everyone propose utopias that is, large-scale planning and to shape the future on that basis."[1] From Jorge Alessandri, who reached the presidency in 1958 and was defeated in 1970 by Salvador Allende, to Augusto Pinochet, the entire Chilean political elite was trapped by the passion for the future and the political economy of the impossible. From the messianic socialism of Allende to the technocratic utopia of the Chicago Boys, the discourse and practice of economics continued to be steeped in a single desire to remove limits, through words and numbers, to economic projects and programs with an eye to the horizon of an imminent revolution, sometimes social, sometimes neo-liberal. Over the course of these densely ideological years, an entire political economy was displayed, sometimes grounded on the arrival of a classless and at times stateless society.

In this sense the 1973 coup d'état and the playbooks of
the Chicago Boys (named for their alma mater, the
University of Chicago) during the first years of the neo-
liberal revolution were not a departure from but rather
another continuous episode in the waltz of paradigms.
Pinochet brought in American ultra-orthodox economists
who, inspired by professorial luminaries such as Milton
Friedman and Arnold Harberger, sought to apply the
textbook theories and restructured the nation's entire
economy. Chile embarked on a pioneering free-market
strategy, a shock therapy obsessed with ideological purity. The majority of Chile's political leaders did not find
their way to a renewed realism until the 1980s. The 1982
debt crisis and the prospect of a referendum in 1988
helped induce this transformation. It was only after the
1982–83 crisis that Chile opted for economic policies that
focused on the possible, for more tailored macroeconomic reforms embedded in realism and pragmatism. Under
pressure from these events, the neo-liberal economic
policies practiced by the Chicago-trained economists
installed by Pinochet were modified. Neo-liberals effectively nationalized the financial system at the beginning
of the 1980s and faced one of the harshest Latin American
banking crises (between 1982 and 1983, GDP fell by 14.5
percent, a national and regional record). The 1985
appointment of Hernán Büchi to lead the reforms and the
support of a new team of economists that included Juan
Andrés Fontaine, at that time Chief Economist at Chile's
central bank, consolidated this more ideologically

flexible orientation. Chile's second wave of Chicago Boys did not hesitate to ignore neo-liberal and monetarist precepts when the country's economic reality demanded it.

In the midst of the decade of Reagan and Thatcher, the country of the Chicago Boys, known as the den of Latin American liberalism, illustrated this pragmatic direction. As the economist Carlos Díaz Alejandro observed, referring to this period, "the clearest example of this paradox is Chile, which, guided by able economists committed to laissez-faire, showed the world yet another road to a de facto socialized banking system."[2] While the leaders of the last two governments of the Pinochet period explored the mysteries of uninhibited reforms, combining neo-liberal sutures and interventionist cures, among the opposition a number of actors engaged in self-criticism and reevaluation of their economic thought as well as their political strategy. The more moderate government sectors, for convenience or due to democratic conviction, adopted more conciliatory strategies, leading the way to a smooth transition that culminated in Pinochet's defeat in the 1988 referendum. In this consultation the Chilean vote in favor of change marked the return to democracy with the 1989 election of Patricio Aylwin, a Christian Democrat, as president of the country.

Chile's great transformation was consolidated with this return to democracy. Chile capitalized on its economic inheritance from the years of dictatorship. In spite of the political shift and the change of regime, it also maintained relative economic continuity. With the fall of the military regime at the end of the 1980s, the Chicago Boys abandoned power. But rather than reject this economic inheritance, Chile's new leaders continued to combine privatization with regulation, trade openness with ongoing state ownership of the mining sector (Codelco), and financial liberalization with capital controls. Finding their country itself flooded with large investment inflows, Chilean policy makers discovered that foreign capital, like good Maipo Valley wine, can be problematic in excess and therefore did not hesitate to impose precedent-setting controls. This control of private capital flows was accomplished through the famous system of *encaje* (the tax system on short-term capital inflows adopted in 1991 and eliminated in 1998, at a time when the entire world looked at this "model" for inspiration on how to stop the contagion of financial crises). In this way what is now called "growth with equity" began to show its pragmatic outlines.

Under the new democratic regime, monetary and fiscal orthodoxy continued in place. In this way the Chilean central bank celebrated its new independence, carefully nurturing the process of gradual deflation. The search for price stability was accompanied by a controlled fiscal policy, while the effort at trade liberalization continued to deepen. In the matter of fiscal competence, the democratic government reestablished a budget surplus (since 1975 interrupted only during the period 1982–1985) and even reinforced this discipline, adopting an implicit surplus norm in an attempt to reduce public debt gradually.

The social component was not neglected, for in 1990, new labor laws restored some of the rights suppressed under the military dictatorship. At the same time, social expenditures in absolute terms and as a percentage of total expenditures increased. The pace of growth, relatively elevated, combined with interventionist social policies, allowing for a significant reduction of poverty: from 45 percent before the restoration of democracy, it shrank to 20 percent among Chileans at the beginning of the current century.

Chile displayed much economic pragmatism in the last two decades, whether before or after the democratic transition. In 1981, under Pinochet, Chile implemented one of the boldest and most innovative reforms: privatization of the government-run retirement system. In this case, too, the spirit and the implementation of reform were steeped in possibilism. In its Chilean version, the system of private retirement accounts, often presented as the archetype of neo-liberal reforms, is a jewel of pragmatism, combining privatization and regulation. Chile's system of private retirement accounts is simultaneously one of neo-liberal inspiration and one of interventionist application, and it has become one of the world's best-regulated economic institutions. The inspiration is clearly neo-liberal, the pension privatization being the creation of labor and social security secretary, José Piñera, a staunch proponent of the free market and a member of the hard-line privatization group known as the Chicago Boys.[3] The implementation of the reform since 1988 has

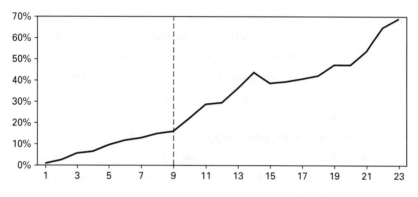

Figure 4.1
Evolution of asset management in Chile's system of pension funds.
Vertical scale: assets managed by pension funds as % of GDP.
Horizontal scale: years after implementation of reform. Source: Banco
Bilbao Vizcaya Argentaria.

been, however, tremendously pragmatic and embedded
in a sophisticated net of norms, constraints, and regulations. For pension funds, the detailed Chilean regulation
established a minimum capital deposit in the system and
a formal separation of these funds from other financial
institutions. Strict rules regulated the assets assigned
to the investment portfolios managed by fund administrators. Originally, investment funds were mainly
restricted to government securities, bank deposits,
investment-grade corporate bonds, and mortgage bonds.
In 2005, however, Administradores de Fondos de
Pensiones (AFPs) invest in many types of investments,
including equity, foreign securities, and real estate, and
diversification toward assets outside Chile is authorized.

Investments in stocks have, however, a maximum limit, as do foreign investments (although, in an effort to allow for greater risk diversification, assets invested outside Chile cannot account for more than one-third of the pension funds' assets).

In addition, Chile's pension system has been improved by successive slight adjustments and readjustments. For instance, in 1985 the option to invest in the stock market was introduced, and in 1992 investing in international capital markets was allowed. As a result of these adjustments, the Chilean system finds itself today less dependent on issuing of bonds by the government. In 2002, government assets yielding regular dividends represented barely one-third of the assets of Chilean retirement funds, in contrast to over 70 percent in Argentina, Mexico, and Bolivia. In Argentina government bonds accounted for the bulk of pensions' assets, so when the country defaulted on its government debt in 2001 it also defaulted on its pensioners. This decreasing dependence on state assets constituted a guarantee in a region where non-payment of government debt is not unusual and confiscation by the State not exceptional, as illustrated by Argentina's default in 2001. This pension reform in particular is an excellent example of the gradual nature of changes to Chile's economic policy over the last decades. This continuity is illustrated in figure 4.1. Beginning in 1990, the year Chile returned to democracy (only 9 years after the implementation of the social security reforms), the asset values in these pension accounts do not decrease but on the contrary shot up: not only were reforms not cancelled but, on the contrary, they were deepened, adopted, and adapted.

Even with these reforms, Chile's pension system is certainly not exempt from shortcomings. Coverage is still far from universal and the rewards for the pensioners not always bright. Studies by the state regulator of the private pension administrators, the Superintendencia de Administradoras de Fondos de Pensiones, conclude that more than one-half of the affiliates of the system will hardly be able to save enough in their pension accounts by retirement to fund even the "minimum pension," which is currently set at about 130 U.S. dollars per month. Another issue is that the volatility of performance exposes these funds to the shocks and counter-shocks of the financial markets. In 1991 the performance of pension funds grew by 30 percent; by 1995 its growth was –2.5 percent. This crisis forced regulators to intervene, pushing forward a new series of reforms—also gradual—designed to soften this financial volatility. But beyond these accomplishments and failures, Chile's reformed pension system has allowed the country to accelerate the accumulation of capital and to approach international standards of accumulation of capital. With assets estimated at 60 percent of GDP, and with annual performances close to a median of 10 percent for the period 1981–2002, the system has shown respectable long-term results.

Although the effect of pension reform on overall savings continues to be a subject of debate in academic circles, empirical studies confirm that pension funds have
contributed to greater liquidity in Chile's relatively narrow capital market. Above all, these reforms have
allowed the development of long-term capital markets,
since pension funds operate with medium-term horizons, with a greater tendency than other financial institutions to conserve assets in their portfolios. The typical
pension fund therefore retains assets in its portfolio for
several years; it looks also for investment opportunities
overseas thought mandates negotiated with asset managers specializing, for example, in European or U.S.
bonds and equities. The Chilean reforms have also fos-
tered imitation in the region. Inspired by the Chilean
pioneering experience, other countries followed suit in
the early 1990s—first Peru, then Argentina and
Colombia. Another eleven Latin American countries
have reformed their national retirement plans over the
last two decades in order to boost the accumulation of
capital in countries traditionally dependent on foreign
savings. This is no small feat in Latin America where the
national savings rate is generally and noticeably inferior
to those of Asia (twice as low as China's in 2005, for
instance). Everywhere in the region, pension systems are
contributing to boost national health. Another issue,
more related to the direct beneficiaries, is the low level of
social coverage—both pensions and the broader array of

safety nets—due to the existence of a large informal sector. In Chile more than half of workers have coverage,
but in most countries the level of coverage rates have
ranged from roughly 10 percent to 60 percent of the economically active population. Mandatory individual
account plans in Latin America have generally failed to
cover more than half of the labor force, and because the
half not covered is the half with lower income, these
plans have failed to address problems of poverty in old
age. Contribution rates also have been high—typically 10
percent of salary. Thus, improving the coverage ratio and
addressing the issue of the low-income segments of the
population remain pending issues. Moreover, adaptation
rather than replication of the Chilean example is needed.
The proponents of pension privatization have suggested
that a single model could be applied to any country; once
again Latin American realities prompted more pragmatic
approaches.

Chile stands out for its success at developing a mixed
political economy. It is one of the most open Latin
American countries with respect to commerce, with a
rate of trade openness that accounted for more than 70
percent of its GDP in 2005. Its customs tariffs are among
the lowest in the world, and it has a worldwide record
number of free-trade agreements, including those recently concluded with the United States, the European
Union, Korea, and China and those pending with India
and Japan. But none of this prevents Chile from keeping a
significant portion of its mining sector, which represents

nearly 40 percent of its total exports, in the hands the State, copper remaining a strategic asset, as do many other commodities in the region (and worldwide—the major oil companies of developing countries remain in state hands, as do PDVSA in Venezuela and Pemex in Mexico).

Another example of pragmatic political economy has been the implementation of a system of capital controls. With the objective of restricting short-term capital inflows, which are accused of causing sudden changes in the exchange rate and of undermining efforts at macro-economic stabilization, at the beginning of the 1990s, the Chilean authorities devised the instrument of *encaje*, which obligates investors to place a percentage of short-term liquidity in a reserve fund. In the case of a rapid withdrawal of funds, investors lose a percentage of their assets held in reserve. This measure was designed to limit the short-term inflow of capital, as well as to foster long-term investments. This Chilean innovation inspired a multitude of projects and thoughts. Malaysian Prime Minister Mahathir Mohamad's flirtation with capital controls dates from 1998, when Malaysia was struggling against the turbulence of Asian financial markets. Many also noted at the time that China, India, and Vietnam, which had capital controls, were relatively unaffected by the crisis. In 2005, in an attempt to discourage "speculative" inflows and to protect the Argentine peso from strengthening further against the dollar, Néstor Kirchner's government implemented similar measures, obliging investors bringing capital into the country to lock away 30 percent of the total amount for 12 months. All around the world the Chilean policies were used as references for cooling down inflows of "hot" (that is, short-term) capital. The efficacy of these policies was widely debated, as were their effects. The capacity of *encaje* to cool down the flow of "hot" capital was questioned, and the criticisms multiplied, especially in light of this measure increasing the cost of credit for small and medium-size businesses. At the beginning of 2000 the *encaje* was set at zero. But once again Chile and its leaders displayed remarkable imagination and pragmatism by inventing a new system of capital control. (It is worth mentioning that as a Ph.D. student Ricardo French-Davis, one of the fathers of the *encaje*, walked the halls of the University of Chicago.)

Less ideological and more consensual, today the political economy of democratic Chile, whether led by Eduardo Frei or Ricardo Lagos, continues in a possibilist style that was outlined in the 1980s and consolidated in the 1990s. It is a style characterized by a degree of skepticism toward pre-established models and toward ideological violence, whether inspired by neo-liberal economics or by interventionist policies. The continuity that Chile's democratic governments have maintained with respect to the more free-market political economy introduced by the military regime, especially in the matter of privatizations and of the neo-liberal direction of previous years, is remarkable. Yet, as we have seen, forced by pragmatism, the new leaders of a democratic Chile did not hesitate to intervene in controlling capital flows, the famous *encaje* of 1991, or to keep a large portion of the copper mining industry in the hands of the State.

In a region marked by financial turbulence, today Chile appears as an island of financial as well as macroeconomic stability. Its relatively austere monetary and fiscal policies constitute solid institutional anchors. Similarly, the country relies on a broad platform of macroeconomic reforms that contribute to confidence in the Chilean economy as manifested by the international investment community. Chile is one of the few Latin American economies to enjoy the international financial market's highest investment rating (the much-praised investment grade) and the only one to have risk premiums far below regional standards. (Mexico, which has the region's other great "investment grade," has risk premiums three times those of Chile.) With respect to trade and financial liberalization, Chile is regarded as an international point of reference, its trade openness in recent years having further buttressed a widely lauded economy. A pioneer in the privatization of the retirement accounts, sanitation services, and educational systems, over recent years the country has persevered in this economic pragmatism. Chile knocked on the door of the Organisation for Economic Cooperation and Development. In its 2003 survey of Chile (the first one dedicated to that country), the OECD rightly noted that stable and gradual economic policies were important to Chile's success.

Also important to Chile's success is a patient and non-dogmatic search for growth. Chile has implemented a political economy of the possible in a way that is free of rigid ideologies. Certainly Chile has lost the luster of the years of high growth, as in recent years its annual growth rate has fallen behind the 5–6 percent annual rate of growth that characterized the period 1984–1997. (The long-term tendency over the last 40 yeas has been 2.5 percent annual growth.) However, the bedrock of past reforms and the solid consensus that animates Chile's political and economic elite also help to sustain a possibilist direction, an eminently pragmatic trajectory in which an ethic of responsibility predominates, rather than an ethic of convictions, as in other times in Chile's history. The Chilean example is not a model or a paradigm to follow; it invites, in fact, the adoption and consequently the adaptation of economic policies designed to address particular situations and tackle specific issues, free of any pre-established scheme. Going against the prevailing current, it also illustrates that a Latin American country can, by virtue of consistency, avoid succumbing to ideological fashions, most of them invented and tailored in the northern hemisphere, and can escape the trap of underdevelopment. Chile is not the region's wealthiest country in natural resources; it does not benefit from any geographical proximity to the world's leading economy; it does not enjoy a vast internal market. In spite of these deficiencies, Chile leads the various Latin American indexes of development and competitiveness, and in 2004 and 2005 its GDP was growing at a rate of 6 percent (with help from an increased external demand, from a boom in copper prices, and from historically low interest rates in the world, but also with the help of its own virtues of skillful macroeconomic management).

The Democracy of the Possible

Like most of its regional neighbors (except Cuba) and its Iberian cousins, Chile offers a robust contradiction to the pessimistic prophecies regarding the impossibility of democracy emerging in Latin America. In the case of Chile, it is more a matter of democracy re-emerging, since the country was already democratic before the 1973 coup d'état. Since the late nineteenth century, a growing number of Chileans of working-class origin could participate in the elections, and subsequent laws only widened enfranchisement. Women's suffrage was introduced in 1931, the same year as in Spain and before France (1944) or Argentina (1949). In the 145 years preceding the 1973 coup (excepting the interruption in 1891 and the civil war that followed, and excepting the turbulent period 1924–1932), Chile experienced only 30 months of interruption of its democratic constitutional norms. In Chile, therefore, as of 1973, the omnipresent memory of a lost democracy to recover became an obsession for the democrats, who lost what they praised most in politics: civil liberties, deliberative spaces, voting rights, and in the end democracy. Chile exemplified a specific political trajectory in which not invention but re-invention of a lost democracy dominated. The democratization was conceived by the Chilean opposition as a return voyage, as the recovery of a tradition of consensus and moderation, diminished by the ideological escalation of the years of Frei and Allende, and brutally interrupted by the military coup.

The Chilean political trajectory shows the extent to which democratization is a matter of rhythms and sequences. Chile's political apprenticeship was extraordinary—its extreme polarizations of the 1960s and the 1970s were succeeded by a search for consensus. As I documented in a 1997 paper, in the course of regaining democracy, what came about was the transformation of a society indifferent to risk, risk-averse, (in the decade of the 1960s and during the early 1970s) to a political community strongly sensitive to it (as of the coup d'état of 1973). To understand the Chilean trajectory is, above all, to calibrate the extraordinary process of political maturity that took place between 1980 and 1989, between the year of the promulgation of the Pinochet constitution and the year of the plebiscite that opened the floodgates to the democratic wave.

Once convinced that the regime was economically and politically rooted, from 1980 to 1989, day by day, the opposition to General Pinochet adapted itself to the timing of the military regime, accepting progressively the times and the terms of the constitution, tailored especially for the dictator. This constitution was a mechanism of political clockwork; not only did it dictate the terms of electoral mandates and the date of the plebiscite (concessions made to national and international pressures), it also attempted to eliminate the coerced time of elective democracy and the sectors involved with the country's institutional life, as in the case of life appointments for senators. (The 2005 revision of the constitution removed life appointment of senators.) Once it became evident that the strategy of fighting against the regime through street riots was an impasse and that the economic collapse of the beginning of the 1980s would not lead to the political collapse of Pinochet's regime, the opposition changed its strategic approach and played the game within the boundaries imposed by the regime. Accepting the plebiscite time constraints imposed by the constitution, the opposition played its own game. As the 1988 plebiscite drew nearer, the strategists of the transition—Edgardo Boeninger, Ricardo Lagos, José Miguel Insulza, Alejandro Foxley, and others belonging to an opposition group comprising Social Democrats and Christian Democrats—reconciled and realized that the plebiscite was an extraordinary opportunity to beat the dictator at his own game. Beyond the fall of the Berlin Wall in 1989, what stands out in this year is that Chile's democrats were not "obstinate in keeping up what is collapsing, or

too hasty in establishing what seems to announce itself"
(as Benjamin Constant said of the French Revolution).[4]
The Chilean transition and its democratic consolidation
were, in this sense, a renunciation of what Hirschman,
using a term from Flaubert's *Madame Bovary*, called the
"rage de vouloir conclure"—the rage to conclude, the
impatience to reach results without proceeding step by
step. Today most actors on the Chilean political stage
know, as did Samuel Beckett's Godot, that democracy in
the absolute sense has not arrived and never will, as it is
a regime of perfectibility and not perfection, and that politics aims not for perfection but is a process of improvement that points toward a horizon of the perfection that
is possible. Chilean possibilists saw, in the return to
democracy and to a democratic life made up of debates,
conflicts, consensus, arguments, and counterarguments,
a reawakening of a political life that had become banal.
This reawakening is not inscribed in the lyric poetry of
revolutionary impulses, but rather in the more contained
prose of the politics of the possible, which is in the end
the grammar of democracy.

5   Lula Light

Another possibilist experience, as singular as Chile's though younger and less articulated, is found in Brazil. Under Fernando Henrique Cardoso, this country also established deeper roots in democratic soil and committed itself to economic pragmatism. The famous Real Plan, welcomed by numerous critics for its successful program of macroeconomic stabilization and fight against hyperinflation, allowed the containment of the inflationary spiral and checked the progress of the country along unknown paths. Implemented in 1994, the Real Plan succeeded in breaking through the inertia of inflation and achieved stability after 30 years of high price volatility deep-rooted in the Brazilian social fabric, this success coming after many earlier failures, such as the Cruzado Plan of 1986, the Bresser Plan of 1987, the summer plan of 1989, and the Collor Plans of 1991 and 1992.

Recent Brazilian history also has been characterized by frustrated democratic experiences, authoritarian interruptions, and the imposition of a social body polarized by forced-march models of industrial policy and by import-substitution policies. The left-wing democratic experience of the period 1946–1964 was a stage in the broader era of Brazilian populism (1930–1964), an era of economic nationalism, state-guided modernization, import substitution, and trade policies. This experience, characterized by a growing populism, nationalism, and developmentalism that contributed to the crisis that gripped Brazil, was ended in 1964 by a right-wing military coup. This government sustained itself until the return to democracy in 1985, situated within the framework of the debt crisis that broke out in Brazil following the onset in Mexico during the early 1980s and by the military regime's inability to control galloping inflation. One of the Brazilian democrats' priorities was to cut short the inflationary spiral by implementing in 1986 a heterodox quick fix of anti-inflationary shocks, the Cruzado Plan, which did not succeed at interrupting the rise in prices. In 1989 after the return to democracy, the first direct presidential elections installed Fernando Collor de Melo. His new heterodox program to fight inflation quickly followed the same fate of its predecessors. His presidency was shortened by his impeachment for corruption, proof that the Latin American zeitgeist had changed not only for the autocrats but also for the apprentice democrats that aspired to perpetuate the corrosive political habits of corruption.

Trade liberalization and the privatization agenda finally saw the light, but was wrapped in a halo of happy skepticism and the lack of urgency characteristic of

Brazil. The arrival of a sociologist, formerly a proponent of State-centered development strategies, as head of the Ministry of Finance in 1993 marked a milestone in the country's economic trajectory, which until then had been particularly troubled. Fernando Henrique Cardoso surrounded himself with a team of young and brilliant technocrats who in 1994 introduced a program of orthodox reforms, as imaginative as they were pragmatic: the Real Plan. Unlike the earlier failed plans, it did not depend on a general price and wage freeze to stop inflation but placed the heart of the measures an audacious de-indexation, reversing the previous policies in which prices and wages were indexed to inflation of the Brazilian economy and the creation of a new monetary unit, the Real. As a result of this stabilization plan, the inflationary fever declined and consumer spending recovered.

This success led the sociologist-turned-financial apprentice to the presidency of Brazil. From that office, Cardoso, who had been one of the gurus of Dependency Theory, moved to more pro-market reforms. He left away his former economic world vision, partly inspired by the Argentine economist Raúl Prebisch, centered on two sets of states, described as dominant (advanced industrial nations) and dependent (which rely heavily on the export of a single commodity for foreign exchange earnings), or center and periphery. Once in government, he started a broad program of pro-market reform and when he was reelected in 1998, he did not hesitate to surround himself with other brilliant technocrats, experienced in the laws of the market. One of them was none other than Arminio Fraga, a talented Wall Street economist trained at Princeton who left George Soros's asset-management firm in New York to become governor of Brazil's central bank.

During the 1990s, under Cardoso, Brazil adopted, through successive moderate measures, economic policies that combined liberal openings with state control. Sustained by several decades of populism and economic nationalism, the opposition disapproved of these timid incursions. Yet opposition leaders did not prevent the 1995 ratification of six proposals by the team under the new Minister of Finance, Pedro Malan, to amend the 1988 constitution to foster more liberal and more rapid economic policies. The main changes were designed to offer foreign businesses investment opportunities in the mining and oil sectors. Foreign companies were also allowed to supply telephone services, to operate in the area of data transmission, and even to distribute natural gas to individuals and businesses. To these measures were added—always gradually—fiscal adjustments and progressive economic liberalizations.

Centralized government and state intervention did not disappear, however. The relaxation of controls on Brazil's state-owned oil industry, Petrobras, in 1995 was only partial, and many tentative reforms were rejected by Parliament. The Asian financial crisis, and the danger of contagion, spurred the rate of reforms at the end of 1997, propelling in a single movement the first serious administrative reforms, along with increased taxes, budget reductions and, most importantly, the establishment of a fund for fiscal stabilization that allowed the federal government to limit the budget overruns of the federated states. Privatization continued, not at the lightening pace enforced in Argentina, but rather as if meted out by an eye dropper. Yet privatization was broadly implemented, as illustrated by the privatization of the telephony holdings of Telebras. All in all the government privatized more than $90 billion worth of government owned enterprises, concluded the sale of industrial and mineral giants, such as the Vale do Rio Doce (CVRD), transferred to the market electric utilities and the railways sector, and sold most of the state government-owned banks. The Russian ruble crisis in the summer of 1998 once again shook Brazil's economy, forcing the Brazilian government, after Cardoso was reelected in October, to impose more fiscal austerity in order to reestablish trust in international capital markets. In January 1999, Brazil's central bank resigned itself to allowing the real, Brazil's currency unit, to float, following the moratorium proclaimed by the Governor of State of Minas Gerais and former Brazilian president Itamar Franco, which itself generated new financial turbulence.

The second Cardoso administration (1999–2003) was for some observers more disappointing than the first. After a slight shudder, the legislative apparatus submerged itself in a kind of lethargy. The government's attention centered on consolidating the achievements of

Cardoso's first term. The fickle nature of growth, however, was confronted by the energy crisis in 2001, and then Argentina's spectacular default.

In spite of these setbacks and its critics, Cardoso's second term was able to consolidate some important victories in regard to fiscal federalism by imposing the law of fiscal responsibility. This legislation was the first in a country with national budget deficits intensified by the federal states. During the 1999 crisis, Minas Gerais, one of the poorest states, declared itself in default to the Brazilian Federation. In the social arena, a series of initiatives that had already been outlined in his first term were reinforced, consolidated and amplified. In particular, programs that transferred resources directly to the most impoverished and allowed them to keep their children in school were established all around the country, on the municipal and state and federal level.

By the end of 2001 the spiraling aftershocks resonating from the Argentine crisis caused the Brazilian economy to stagger again, with debt at the epicenter of its financial worries in 2002. Suddenly, starting in April, as the candidacy of Luiz Inácio Lula da Silva coalesced, the international financial markets focused on the presidential elections scheduled for October 2002. The fear of an overtly leftist government, stereotypically synonymous with monetary disorder and the relaxation of fiscal discipline, added to the growing unease of the international capital markets. Over a few weeks, exchange rates and risk premiums registered ample swings, and the investors' nervousness grew exponentially as the electoral polls confirmed the likelihood of success for the leader of the Workers' Party, Lula. In October 2002, when Lula was elected Brazil's 39th president, the aversion of the financial markets peaked and risk premiums reached unprecedented levels: 2,500 basis points (they were multiplied by 5), an "achievement" equaled only by ten countries in the history of emerging markets. Brazil's public debt reached a record of 65 percent of GDP, while the real depreciated by nearly 50 percent.

Lula's rise to power constituted a major watershed event in two respects. First, it confirmed Brazil's democratic consolidation. The transfer of power between Cardoso and Lula was itself a lesson in political elegance. For the first time in the history of Brazil's contemporary democracy, the world's fourth-largest democracy but also its third most unequal country, elected a president from its working class, born in poverty who rose from a shoeshine boy to a trade-union leader and founder of the Workers' Party, the largest left-wing force in Latin America. After competing in four presidential elections, by winning over 61 percent of the popular votes, Lula became president of Brazil in October 2002.

Added to this electoral victory was a second one the following year, 2003. Defying all expectations, Lula regained the confidence of the international financial markets. Their fears did not materialize, and Lula stuck to his pre-campaign promises of market-friendly reforms. In 2002 the fever of the financial operators, especially foreign ones, and the worsening of Brazilian spreads, that is risk premiums over U.S. Treasury Bills, had dominated the landscape. The year 2002 was characterized by escalating risk premiums, that rose exponentially as Lula rose in the polls and his chances for election became more likely. This same phenomenon of escalating risk premiums in anticipation of Lula being elected president was a constant in Lula's four presidential bids in the elections of 1989, 1998, and especially 1994 and 2002, as figure 5.1 shows. In his last 2002 attempt Lula had been at pains to convince investors that he had abandoned his earlier far-left views on touchy subjects like foreign debt. Nevertheless, and countering the darkest Wall Street prophecies, the newly elected Lula turned out to be surprisingly pragmatic in his economic policies. He changed his tune after he took office and endorsed mainstream measures opting for gradualism, combining fiscal austerity and tight monetary policy with social activism. Dubbed "Lula Light," he soon became the darling of investors and financial markets while he was jeered at during the anti-globalization World Forum in Porto Alegre in 2004.

Within months, the Brazilian real grew stronger, and stabilized in a lasting way. Brazilian bond yields compared to U.S. yields on federal government bonds improved and spreads returned to levels not exceeding 500 basis points. Interest rates began to fall in the second half of 2003, from 26 percent to 17 percent in the course of a few months. Directors appointed to Brazil's Ministry of Finance and the central bank appeased the markets, which were gradually convinced that Lula's new administration intended to sustain the direction of fiscal and monetary orthodoxy begun by Cardoso. In fact, Lula and his supporters were careful to abandon the rhetoric of abrupt change, tainted as it is by messianic dreams and impossible utopian promises invoked during the presidential campaign. However, and in spite of all the efforts deployed, during the campaign they had not been able to convince the international financial markets, which remained skeptical after the election. Yet once Lula's cabinet was established, the financial team led by technocrats, gifted with remarkable political tact. Minister of Finance Antonio Palocci—a former Trotskyite, trained as a medical doctor, who cut his political teeth as mayor of Ribeirão Preto, a medium-size city in the interior of São Paulo State—emerged as an even-keeled pragmatist. He impressed financial markets by pledging that Brazil would follow sound financial policies and promptly displayed its orthodox vision of economic development based on two anchors of credibility: controlling inflation on the monetary front, and solid budgetary discipline on the fiscal side. In the end Palocci administered an even harsher dose of austerity than his long-serving predecessor, Pedro Malan, a respected orthodox economist who was a favorite target of the Workers' Party while sitting in opposition.

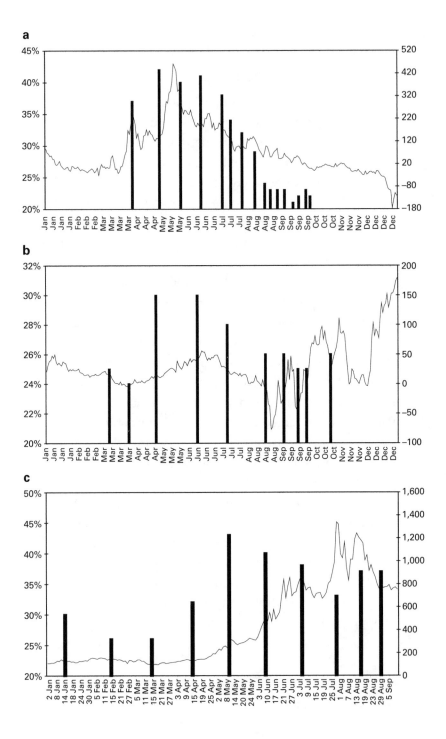

Elections and Financial Markets: The Lula Effect

In less than a year, Lula's administration passed reforms that had been proposed unsuccessfully by his predecessor. Social security measures that Cardoso had attempted to enact during his 45 months in office were approved in less than 12 months, a record speed. (See table 5.1.)

Reforms involving pensions sparked massive protests in 2003. Brazil's retirement system reforms, however, were directly in line with the preceding government's strategy. Lula and his supporters had originally opposed these attempts while in the opposition, but unhesitatingly adopted these strategies once they were in power, propelling this initiative to the top of the economic policy agenda in 2003. In contrast to other Latin American countries, these reforms did not affect the basic principles of the distribution system—the changes avoided tackling delicate issues like reforming in depth the public pension system and only achieved impressive improvements in private pensions. Reforms included raising the retirement age and also introduced more marginal changes in the public systems, such as limiting civil servants' pensions. Yet in Brazil there was no radical transfer of the public realm to the private sector, no privatization of

Figure 5.1
Differential of spreads between the Emerging Market Bond Index (EMBI) of Brazil and the general EMBI and the intention to vote for of Lula (in %; left scale) in (a) 1994, (b) 1998, and (c) 2002. Right scale: spreads in basis points. Source: Santiso and Martínez 2003.

Table 5.1
Time elapsed until approval of constitutional amendments passed by Brazil's Congress during Cardoso's first term (1994–1998). Estimates based on data from Crédit Suisse, First Boston (CSFB), and Brazilian Congress.

Amendment	First vote	Last vote	Number of months
Administrative reform	September 26, 1995	March 11, 1998	30
Social Security reform	April 24, 1995	December 15, 1998	44
Reelection	April 26, 1995	June 4, 1997	26
Reform based on fiscal stabilization	August 30, 1995	February 29, 1996	7
Reintroduction of CPMF [a] tax	August 30, 1995	July 24, 1996	11

a. Contribuição Provisónia sobre Movimentação su Transmissão de Valores e de Créditos e Direitor de Naturaleza Financeira. This tax was created in 1996.

pension funds like in Chile. In Brazil the state preserved control of its ability to secure the future of citizens.

The reticence of public functionaries, combined with that of elected representatives, moderated the scope of the pension reforms. With respect to the general pension system, the calculation of the total value of pensions was modified to consider an average of 80 percent of an individual's best salary years since 1994, and not only an average of the last four years, as done previously. The idea of imposing a minimum retirement age was finally discarded due to massive opposition. While Cardoso was unable to overcome the resistance of Parliament and of the Workers' Party, Lula initiated reforms of the government employees' retirement system. In less than eight months, the constitutional amendments were ratified, again, a record speed for reforms in Brazil. With this passage, the retirement age for government employees was set at 60 years for men and 55 years for women, in combination with a minimum term in their public service in order to merit a pension equivalent to their last year's earned salary, while personal contributions to the retirement fund was set at 11 percent of the salaries of government employees.

These were reform measures taken in spite of great reticence, often even at the heart of the governmental coalition, thanks to a leadership style that is both flexible and firm. Lula, a seasoned union negotiator, is a master of all persuasive arts, from war in the legislative trenches to negotiations among dockworkers. He has been firm, combining concessions with maintaining priorities, displaying unquestionable political courage by courting displeasure among his own bastions of support.

Another large reform took place in the fiscal realm, centered mainly on improved tax collection and spending controls. The guiding principle was to guarantee the fundamental task of increasing and controlling government revenues. However, so as not to confront the powerful state governors, taxes on necessary goods and the enactment of unified tax rates on the sale of merchandise and services (a kind of value-added tax) were postponed.

Improving education, sanitation, and the minimum wage, the social emphasis of Lula's government was not neglected. But in order to sustain a direction of fiscal austerity and to inhibit any risk of an inflationary slide, exchange rates were kept deliberately high during the first six months of Lula's presidency. It was also for the new government to show its pro-market credentials and secure its post election credibility toward financial markets. Along with this, the objective of achieving a budget surplus was reinforced and the government scrupulously respected its commitments to the International Monetary Fund. Toward the end of 2003, not only was the inflation rate low, but net public debt also fell below the threshold of 56 percent of GDP, tumbling from levels of 65 percent at the peak of the 2002 crisis. The price of this orthodoxy was, however, that in 2003 there was almost no economic growth. The radical wing of the Workers' Party, which considered Lula's measures too orthodox, became unhappy.

However, at the end of 2003 Lula's poll numbers were high, and a political economy of patience gradually took root. The population was eager to give Lula and his administration time to enact these changes. According to the polls, 60 percent then approved of the personal achievements of their president, a record with respect to the weak hold leaders have upon political power in Brazil, as is true throughout Latin America. In addition, macroeconomic data consolidated Brazilians' relative satisfaction, since in 2004, the economy achieved an annual growth rate close to 5 percent, clearly above the preceding 20-year average of 2.7 percent annual growth. The trade balance, due in part to the pull of soaring Chinese demand, registered a record surplus in 2004 and 2005, and exports passed the $100 billion threshold, more than 15 percent of GDP.

The most remarkable feature of Brazil's economic evolution lies in the diversification of products it makes and markets for export. The charts below, which gather the Herfindahl-Hirschman indexes (a commonly accepted measure of market concentration or diversification calculated by squaring the market share of each product competing in the market and then adding the resulting numbers) of Brazilian exports, by product as well as by

a

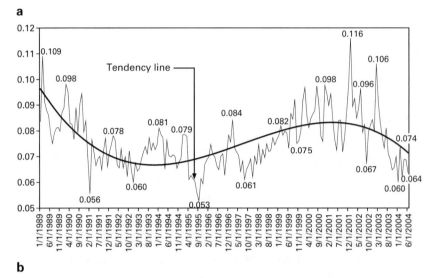

b

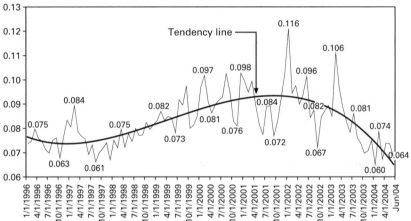

Figure 5.2
Index of concentration of Brazil's exports, 1996–2004, (a) by products
and (b) by markets. Source: Bradesco 2004.

market, show that these last tend toward zero. The index takes into account the relative size and distribution of the exports and approaches zero when these are fully diversified. Exports are already less concentrated than they were in the 1990s, in terms of products as well as of markets.

This openness is not only about trade. Brazilian corporations are increasing their sales overseas but also pushing their expansion abroad, led by Petrobras, which bought Argentina's largest independent oil company in 2002. In 2004, Brazilian companies invested around $10 billion abroad, a dramatic yearly jump (3,700 percent) for a country that over the previous decades had hardly invested more than $3 billion a year abroad. As in the case of their Mexican counterparts, most of the Brazilian *multilatinas* (Latin multinationals) are building their international expansion investing mainly in other Latin American markets. In the last 3 years, Brazilian companies bought major Argentine companies that were undervalued, including the Quilmes brewery, the oil company Pérez Companc, the steelmaker Acindar, and the cement producer Loma Negra. Brazil's national oil company, Petrobras, spread out to Argentina, Bolivia, and Venezuela. The cellulose producer Aracruz, the iron mining company CVRD, the conglomerate Votorantim, the steelmaker Gerdau, and the agro-industry company Sadia belong to this elite group of Brazilian companies that expanded beyond their home base. Some are already looking to China and to other markets.

Social Policies

Brazil's new leaders devoted attention to the country's endemic social ills, particularly poverty. The fight against poverty became a priority under the presidency of Luiz Inácio da Silva (2003–2006), with a special focus on eliminating hunger in Brazil's most deprived regions. Cardoso used to say that Brazil was not a poor country but rather an unjust country: in spite of a relatively high per-capita GDP, extreme poverty affects 15 percent of the total population, and poverty in general affects over 35 percent of Brazilians. As Latin America's largest economy, Brazil also exemplifies one of the most lopsided income gaps in the world. According to the Brazil-based Applied Economic Research Institute (Instituto de Pesquisa Econômica Aplicada, IPEA), the richest 1 percent of the population controls 13 percent of the nation's wealth, while the poorest 50 percent controls only 13 percent. Lula rightly attempted to convert the scandal of poverty into the priority among Brazil's economic policies, launching the Zero Hunger Program in January 2003. It tried to target malnutrition by introducing a voucher system to be used for buying food that would require children of poor families to remain in school.

Macroeconomic realities and budget constraints and the pharaonic scale and long-term dimension of the challenge forced redistributive tendencies to blur, in spite of Lula's vehement support for these measures while his party was in the opposition. In some ways the macroeconomic policy objectives crowded out part of the domestic social agenda, and never totally reached macroeconomic stabilization, impeding the deployment of all the major initial promises and goals. By the end of Lula's term, many of the initial efforts and enthusiasm had been diverted and wasted through the corruption crisis that rocked the government in 2005, a year before the end of his term. Some of Lula's closest allies were accused of mastering an epic scheme of bribes that sent Brazil into one of its worst political crises since the 1992 impeachment of President Collor for corruption.

As for corruption scandals, the realization of the importance of the capacity and effectiveness of a democratic regime to redistribute income, propelled in the past by a sociologist and today by a labor union leader, is not exactly new in Brazil. It is, however, healthier inasmuch as it is part of a pragmatic political economy, a possibilist push that seeks to detach itself from all ideological noise and is particularly conscious of the fact that democracies survive in prosperous societies, or in the most extreme cases regardless of the income level, as long as per-capita income is distributed in a sufficiently egalitarian manner. In fact, during the second half of the twentieth century, the probability of the "death" of democracies was one in twelve in countries with per-capita income below $1,000 and one in 60 in cases of per-capita income exceeding $6,000. To this is added an ever more remarkable fact, underlined by Przeworski et al.: this "frontier" threshold is around $6,000 in terms of per-capita income, beyond which the possibilities of the survival of democracy are greater, going up when the differences in income are narrower. In other words, democracy's chances for survival are much better when societies are more egalitarian in terms of wealth redistribution.

This combination of economic orthodoxy and social policies was, at any rate, the trademark of the first steps of Lula's administration dominated by a president more attentive to global objectives of sound, equitable and sustainable development than to the ideological purity of the methods used to achieve them. Lula himself insists that he is, above all, a negotiator and not an ideologue. The government officials responsible for the economic portfolios also subscribe to the same empirical line, including Minister of Finance Antonio Palocci, Minister of Planning Guido Mantega, and Minister of Development, Industry, and External Commerce Luiz Furlan (previously president of the board of Sadia, one of Brazil's largest food-processing companies). It is nevertheless true that Brazilian political economy continues to be imbued with a certain "nominal heroism," where individual personality still matters more than institutional authority, and the enactment of these policies to a large degree still depends more on the people in power than on the institutions themselves. Although nominalism may still prevail, Brazil, like Chile, appears to be on a solid path to greater institutional anchoring.

It is obvious that these mixed economic policies are part of the same impulse criss-crossing Latin America—

whether Portuguese-speaking or Spanish-speaking—the creole mixture of thought cross-pollinated by historians and anthropologists, economists and sociologists. In Brazil, where the census registers 136 variations of skin color, the ability to assimilate opposites and to assemble combinations is the anchor foundation of a tropical social pragmatism. "Order and Progress," the motto adopted by the Brazilian republic at its birth in 1889, was one of the favorite proverbs of positivism, inspired directly by Auguste Comte. It combines the will to project into the future with imposing present order upon that projection, to frame it rationally.

"I am a Tupi who plays the lute," wrote the Brazilian poet Mario de Andrade, evoking the reality of a country with multiple allegiances and lineage, where commitments and adaptations are inextricably tangled. Like Andrade's speaker in the poem, Brazilian leaders at the end of the twentieth century and in this new babbling century, are multiplying the combinations. They have become economic lute players without equal, who simultaneously perform great musical operas and the simple music of chance. Planning and imagination, rigor and flexibility mix thus, giving birth on Brazilian soil to yet another variant of the political economy of the possible.

As Chile did in 1989 with its return to democracy, and as Mexico did in 2000 with the election of Fox, in 2002 Brazil experienced a fundamental transition with the election of Lula. In 1989, Chileans opted for economic gradualism instead of another breakdown of all previous reforms, in spite of the dramatic change of political regime. A decade later, the triumph of Mexico's opposition did not end in a disruptive economic discontinuity, rather the contrary. In the same way, Lula became a reference point, maintaining macroeconomic stability, espousing market friendly policies, and advancing social reforms in an unequal and socially polarized region. His administration won approval for bills that had been delayed for years, managing to pass fiscal and pension reforms as well as a new bankruptcy law and a constitutional reform aimed at improving the deficient judicial system.

But an equally important event in Brazil has been the consolidation of what Arminio Fraga has called the new economic regime. This term indicates a more credible political economy, one more centered on achieving a reasonable and ordered goal. In demonstrating to the world that the election of economic policy measures is shared by a very broad spectrum that encompasses elites as well as the masses, and that this choice is derived from pragmatic positions and not from ideological ones, Lula's Brazil too rises, in a singular way, to the possibilism emergent in America.

6   Mexico: The Great Transformation

One of the most lucid essays written about Mexico is not a product of the wise statistical ruminations of a sociologist, the balanced suppositions of a political scientist, or the technical regressions of an economist, but rather of the thoughts of a poet who also was one of the great essayists of his country and of his century, the Nobel Laureate Octavio Paz.

In his 1970 afterword to a new edition of his book *The Labyrinth of Solitude*, Paz describes the extent to which the modern political matrix of his country resides in its will, reiterated every 6 years, to erase the legacy of the previous government. Like the Aztec emperors who with an ever-greater pyramid covered the earlier pyramids built by their predecessors, during the twentieth century Mexico's presidents have insisted on laying waste to the near past. In spite of belonging to the same partisan dynasty, for decades each new president tried to differentiate his new reign from his immediate predecessor in successive autonomous gestures in order to consolidate his authority not only over the State but also over the party: for a limited term of 6 years (a sexenio), the Mexican president was, like the ancient Tlatoani, the absolute political authority and did not tolerate any eclipse of his shining power. Mexico's modern times are composed of mixed temporalities, the present being the confluence of hidden pasts and frustrated futures, a series of subverted Edens that Mexicans simultaneously wish to recover and to forget. In this country of multiple concurrent temporalities, the past, present, and future rub elbows and confront each other. The avenues of Mexico's urbane and peaceful capital are named Insurgentes and Reforma, typically referenced to the Mexican Revolution. The futurist skyscrapers border on the shantytowns, and pre-Columbian pyramids are next to Baroque cathedrals and high-tech corporate headquarters. The name of the party that dominated the political life of the country for more than 70 years, the Institutional Revolutionary Party (Partido Revolucionario Institucional, PRI) juxtaposes and embraces apparently irreconcilable terms that simultaneously promise a radical rupture and a return to a utopian past, while at the same time enacting a conservative present.

To begin with, modern Mexico has been dominated by the eclecticism and pragmatism of the PRI, which adopted simultaneously a conservative and a liberal political economy, both revolutionary and traditionalist, alternating between interventionism and laissez faire policies. Another fine observer of the realities of his country, the novelist Carlos Fuentes, wrote: "Official Mexican political eclecticism was as contradictory, and as fascinating, as the images of the Virgin of Guadalupe that festooned the sombreros of Zapatista guerrillas who, with nothing sacred in mind, assaulted the rural churches of Morelos."[1] It was this pragmatism that allowed PRI leaders to stay in power for nearly 50 years, following the formal establishment of the party in 1946 (70 years, if we trace the origins of the movement that eventually became the PRI to the early 1930s), and to consolidate an unprecedented political stability in Latin America. One of the keys to the relative economic growth and prosperity that the country experienced was this stability, which fell outside the margins of Mexico's own political history from the nineteenth century until Porfirio Díaz rose to power (1876–1880 and 1884–1911), and then until the 1920s. Between 1821 and 1867, Mexico effectively had a total of 56 different administrations. This contrasts with the United States, which had only 13 different administrations between 1817 and 1869. Historians estimate that Mexico's political instability during the four decades following its independence in 1810 cut short the country's growth by 50–100 percent. The political stability of the Porfiriato's Belle Époque near the end of the nineteenth century accounted for 50–88 percent of the increase in growth registered during this period.

Mexico stood outside the frame of all other trajectories in Latin America and displayed surprising political stability during the twentieth century, in contrast to other

countries in the region. After the revolutionary storms of
the 1910s and the stabilization of the regime in 1934
under Lázaro Cárdenas (1934–1940), the country experienced regular presidential successions, a total of 13 if we
count the July 2006 presidential election. But Mexico did
not escape the wear of time. In 2000, for the first time in
the country's recent history, a president from the opposition came to power, ratifying the PRI's slowly eroding
power that began with the 1982 debt crisis that ended the
economic expansion called "the Mexican miracle." The
gradual arrival of an open society between the 1970s and
2000 was a particularly incremental process. The political
calendar started accelerating in 1997, the year in which
the regional elections ratified the shift of government
power to the opposition in a number of states, in the
lower chamber, a portion of the Senate, and, for the first
time, in the mayoralty of tentacular Mexico City. Three
years later the old PRI was evicted from the presidency.
Throughout the entire country a "democratic tradition,"
whose past reached back to the ephemeral government
of Francisco Madero in 1911, was reestablished.

Parallel to this invention of democracy over the last
two decades, Mexico turned toward the modern times of
the market economy. Heirs of Lázaro Cárdenas—who in
the 1930s organized collectivist-inspired agrarian reform
(the *ejido*), and proceeded to nationalize the oil industry—the presidents from the PRI continued their revolutionary task guided by a relatively flexible ideology; laws

were adapted and varied according to the needs of the
moment. Between 1940 and 1980, while its Latin
American neighbors remained trapped in revolutionary
regimes or suffered military coups, Mexico's economy
displayed an enviable cruising speed, with an annual
GDP growth rate of 6 percent. With escalating economic
and political demands, including the emergence of new
social agents and new economic claims, the political system began to get lazy. The PRI's flagrant inability to
respond to these challenges became evident with the
Tlatelolco massacre in October 1968 immediately preceding the 1968 Olympic Games, prompted by the protests
in Mexico echoing student demonstrations and riots all
over the world. The populist pragmatism of leaders in
the 1970s was not able to stem the citizens' escalating
demands and discontent. The great illusion of internal
development shattered in 1982, a landmark year when
Mexico, until then the beneficiary of the oil boom, found
itself at the edge of bankruptcy and the growth miracle
turned into a nightmare. Overnight, the fall in oil prices
deprived it of valuable liquidity. Unable to make good on
its colossal debt, Mexico declared itself in default, inau-
gurating a financial crisis that, like an expansive tidal
wave, submerged all of Latin America. One after another, Latin American countries tumbled into the debt trap.
(Colombia was an exception.) The crisis simmered for the
next 7 years as slow growth, inflation and capital flight
plagued Latin American debtor nations, transforming
the 1980s into a "lost decade."

In 1989, under the Brady Plan, Mexico was able to return to the international capital markets. The crisis definitively concluded with the retirement, 20 years after the debt crisis exploded, of the last Brady bonds, named after Nicholas Brady, the U.S. Treasury Secretary who implemented the 1989 rescue plan that helped Latin American countries regain access to international capital markets by coupling economic reform with debt reduction.

In the meantime, the PRI leadership committed the country to a path of liberal reforms inspired by free-market principles, always with a pragmatic bent and a social touch, which continued to be distinguishing traits of Mexico's economic policy. Under President Miguel de la Madrid (1982–1988), the country aligned itself with the General Agreement on Trade and Tariffs (GATT, the predecessor of the World Trade Organization). In 1988, the PRI candidate, Carlos Salinas de Gortari, won the hotly disputed presidential elections amid an electoral scandal. Forced to legitimize his government quickly, he accelerated the rhythm of reforms initiated by his predecessor, stabilized an economy that had hit bottom in the 1980s, decapitated the oil workers union, and embarked on a series of ambitious macroeconomic reforms that completed those initiated by President Miguel de la Madrid. Under the leadership of a dream team of technocrats with solid academic credentials and backgrounds, including Pedro Aspe and José Serra Puche, the country opened further to the global economy. Mexico signed a historic free-trade agreement, the famous

NAFTA, with the United States and Canada (the world's first between a developing country and developed countries) and dismantled a great portion of the state-run economy through broad privatization programs. The then powers that be went as far as to modify the sacrosanct 1917 constitution, amending article 27 related to the collective agrarian system of the *ejido*—that is, communal property—and substantially modifying communal land ownership. In only a few years, the Mexican economic landscape was transformed, and with it, the country's economy. The struggle against inflation emerged at the head of the proposed reforms. In the meantime, the engineers of this economic acceleration took care to grease the social machinery with a powerful redistributive social program called Solidaridad.

This economic transformation, however, aggravated regional economic disparities. In the southern region of Chiapas, the indigenous people remained on the land and watched as the northern half of Mexico moved away at great speed, pulled by the engine of reforms. On January 1, 1994, while the country's leaders imagined joining the advanced First World with the official enactment of NAFTA, the free-trade agreement with the United States and Canada, the Indians of the Chiapas jungles revolted, led by a postmodern sub-commander who went by the sole war name of Marcos and who was addicted to the Internet rather than to guns, and to words rather than bullets. At the heart of the state apparatus, privatizations weakened the capacity of a government that could no longer feed, as in the past, the system of patronage known as *clientelismo*, while the reformers and the conservative groups in the PRI confronted each other openly. The splits and schisms multiplied, as in 1987, which later led to the rise of a new political actor, the Party of the Democratic Revolution (PRD, Partido de la Revolución Democrática), founded among others by Cuauhtémoc Cárdenas and by Andrés Manuel López Obrador, a leader who became mayor of Mexico City and in 2006 lost the presidential elections.

Financial Markets and Emerging Democracies

In many regards, 1994 was an exceptional year that deserves our lingering attention for a few moments because it illustrates the tensions between financial markets and emerging democracies. These tensions are common to the so-called emerging markets as a whole, and are patently illustrated by Mexico's "Tequila Crisis" of 1994. This crisis spread very quickly to the principal Latin American economies, putting the brakes on the region's overall reform process. Each affected country was forced to interrupt its race toward growth and to adopt drastic measures to stop the financial gangrene from spreading throughout the entire economy and social body. This crisis, called the "tequila effect," also illustrated the ability of Latin America's governments to react and to adapt their free-trade road maps to their particular circumstances and priorities. So, for instance, at the beginning of 1995, Brazil rushed to raise its customs tariffs in spite of the provisions in Mercosur's trade agreement, exemplifying in this way the pragmatic extremes that the Brazilian leaders continue to display.

More than anything else, the 1994 Mexican financial crisis illustrates the temporal conflicts between states and markets, as, above all, it was a short-term liquidity crisis. The prelude to the crisis started in March 1994 with the assassination of the PRI presidential candidate, Luis Donaldo Colosio, in the aftermath of which a crisis of confidence occurred, inducing volatility in the peso's exchange-rate and risk spreads. To cope with this, the Mexican government turned to issuing short-term Treasury bonds as a guarantee against the danger of fluctuating exchange rates. These *tesobonos* were renamed *malditosbonos* (damned bonds) when in December 1994 the authorities were forced to allow the peso to float, a decision which precipitated the crisis. A race ensued between the overreaction of the financial markets and the urgent economic policy measures then underway (injections of approximately $50 billion by the United States and the international financial community, at the beginning of 1995) in order to stem the drain of capital and restore stability in foreign exchange rates. In the course of a few weeks, the value of the tesobonos went from less than 10 percent of public debt on paper to accounting for over 60 percent, activating a financial time bomb that exploded at the end of 1994, once this decline was made public.

The States then attempted to react swiftly, to adjust the timing of their actions and reactions. Put in another way, Latin American governments attempted to adjust their political timetables to the high-speed rhythm of the financial markets. At the same time, other countries increased the speed of their reaction, as the United States did during the Tequila Crisis. Mexico has been particularly helped by the fast reaction of the United States, the propensity of the American chief executive to react quickly being correlated with American interests in Mexico. Before the Tequila Crisis, most mutual and pension funds had been putting money into Mexico, so indirectly a lot of American citizens had assets in the emerging economy immediately south of the border. As Lawrence Broz has shown, members of the US Congress were more or less inclined to support the Mexican rescue package (and later others) depending on the presence of high-skilled voters living in their districts—the constituency that sees real income gains from globalization and financial rescues—or campaign contributions from international banks located in their districts. With the Mexican crisis the international financial system also adjusted its reaction time, introducing new measures that authorized ever-quicker disbursements on the part of the International Monetary Fund. In this way the International Monetary Fund's decision-making mechanisms established urgent procedures to shorten the implementations of those decisions, as well as the time lapse between the experts' missions and the delivery of the final report to the organization's principal decision-making entities (this delay dropped from 90 days to less than 20 days).

In essence, the 1994 Mexican crisis that engulfed Latin America underscores the extent to which economic and political timing interacts. The Tequila Crisis revealed the limits of the short-term logic applied to financial markets and to emerging markets in particular, but also to the state apparatus that adjusted to the accelerations of the markets by implementing short-term solutions. This tendency was shown by the strong concentration of short-term debt, the tesobonos in the case of Mexico that matured in early 1995 (an amount close to $30 million of these bonds were issued, of which one-third was due in the first months of 1995). This example illustrates the delaying tactics States sometimes use in order to proceed, in the desired timeframe, to the necessary adjustments. Why, in fact, wait nine months to undertake the devaluation that had already become necessary by March but was only fully acknowledged in December? In the Mexican case, the looming presidential elections in July 1994 prompted the earlier rejection of a drastic peso adjustment that could have endangered the victory of the PRI candidate, Ernesto Zedillo. A devaluation implied exposure to the risk of losing precious support within the electorate, since the PRI's solid electoral gains were to a great extent achieved from price and exchange-rate stability. In addition, the political and social memory of prior devaluations and the deeply rooted idea that "a

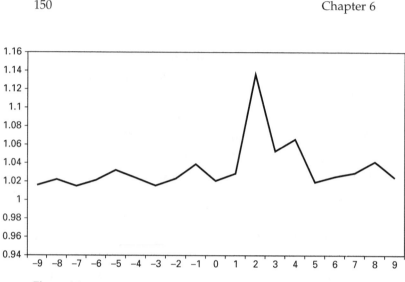

Figure 6.1
Timing of exchange-rate crises and presidential elections in Latin
America, 1970–2000. Horizontal axis: months before and after election.
Vertical axis: exchange-rate depreciation (1.1 represents 10% deprecia-
tion). Source: Frieden and Stein 2001.

president who devalues is a president devalued," as former president José López Portillo pointed out in 1982,
reinforced the conviction it was necessary to seek to gain
time until after the elections.

As Brazil shows, these cardiac crises are not, unfortu-
nately, the exclusive province of the Mexicans. In Latin
America, the timing appears singularly synchronized
with the region's political cycles, particularly with presidential elections. In fact, all of Latin America's great economic and financial crises during the 1990s and first half
of the 2000s—including the 1994 Mexican crisis, the
devaluation of the Brazilian real at the beginning of 1999

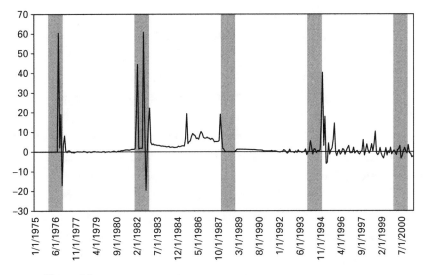

Figure 6.2
Timing of elections and crises in Mexico, 1970–2000. Vertical axis:
exchange-rate variations (%). Source: Santiso and Blázquez 2004.

(a few months after the election of Cardoso), and the crisis of 2002 (when Lula was running for office)—coincid-
ed with presidential elections. During the period
1970–2000, more than 75 percent of the episodes of financial turbulence and exchange-rate crises lasting between
one and five months took place in Latin America following a presidential election. The emergence of Latin
American democracies was marked by ample variations
in risk aversion on the part of the international financial
community operators when approaching electoral
events.

Mexico offers an extreme illustration of this synchronization of political and economic cycles. In this country, the crises have in fact happened with metronomic regularity. The elections of 1976, 1982, 1988, and 1994 all gave rise to financial shocks, debt crises, and banking crises of considerable weight. The decoupling of Mexico's economic cycles from political cycles occurred with the 2000 presidential election, the outgoing administration led by Ernesto Zedillo and his Finance Minister Angel Gurría managing a transfer of power without turbulence. As figure 6.2 shows, before 2000 the monthly exchange-rate fluctuations had tended to increase in presidential-election years (highlighted in gray). One of the paradoxes of Mexico is how it has experienced one of the most regular cycles of economic and financial crises in the world, since every 6 years the Mexican economy has suffered from the turbulence generated in the wake of its presidential election. From this point of view, the year 2000 constitutes a landmark. For the first time in Mexico's recent history, the presidential election result was not accompanied by financial turbulence. Not only was the recurring correlation between its economic and the political cycles altered, but the country also experienced a political transition of primary magnitude. For the first time in 70 years, the political party in power ceded the presidency to a member of the opposition. The financial markets celebrated this velvet Mexican transition with unbounded monetary enthusiasm. The peso did not tumble. Mexican risk premiums declined progressively, while the international rating agencies promptly granted Mexico the most coveted investment grade.

From the Tequila Effect to the Sangrita Effect

In the course of a few years, Mexico traveled the path encompassing the essential vices and virtues of international finance. Lost in the labyrinth of radically shifting anticipations taking place on Wall Street, the country knew, successively, paradise, hell, and the purgatory of the financial markets. Looking back, what stands out is Mexico's extraordinary recovery since the 1994 crisis. The aftermath of this crisis contrasted sharply with the crisis of 1982, which was followed by international financial ostracism for nearly 7 years. Fourteen years later, barely 7 months were needed for the country to return to the international capital markets and for Wall Street to place its bets on this "Brave New World" which in its eyes Mexico had become. In the wake of the American bailout agreement (transformed due to the crisis and the resulting massive infusion of liquidity into a kind of insurance against all risk), Mexico achieved a rapid macroeconomic recovery, firmly hooking the wagon of Mexican growth to the engine of the United States.

The 1997 parliamentary elections affirmed Mexico's renewal in the eyes of international investors. Within Mexico, the stock market celebrated the definitive arrival of the democratic era with gains. The moderation of the declarations that followed the excesses of the campaign were surprising. The return to moderation was attributable to both endogenous and exogenous factors. In effect, the rescue plan was prompted, directed, and impelled by American leaders who wished to stabilize their neighbor to the south as quickly as possible at a time when the United States was anticipating its own presidential election and millions of small savers were caught in the Mexican trap through mutual funds and pension funds. These international factors, together with the economic expansion that the United States was then experiencing, go far toward explaining Mexico's speedy recovery from the 1994 crisis.

Mexico: An (Ex-) Emerging Economy?

Mexico's leaders also were up to the challenge. The Mexico of the "institutionalized revolution" illustrates in many respects a quiet and silent revolution, made up of slow pragmatism and possibilist accelerations. Gradually, reform after reform, crisis after crisis, the economy has slowly achieved a great transformation of its productive machinery, a transformation that doesn't have many equivalents in emerging countries. As we have seen, this great macroeconomic transformation brought with it Mexico's attainment of the best investment grade granted by three rating agencies in the years 2000 and 2001. Mexico has thus been integrated into the very selective global club of investment grade emerging markets that among Latin America's main economies

Table 6.1
Correlations between Mexican and Latin American spreads. Source:
Rigobón 2002.

	2 years earlier[a]	1 year earlier[a]	1 year later
Argentina	88.33%	88.32%	32.42%
Brazil	95.34%	91.13%	66.26%
Colombia	76.33%	87.45%	33.58%
Venezuela	79.13%	89.12%	74.87%
EMBI+[b]	96.96%	93.9%	73.34%

a. From Moody's upgrade to Investment Grade, March 7, 2000.

b. The Emergency Bond Market Index is a benchmark produced by J.
P. Morgan and used by financial industry to measure risk premium.
The EMBI+ is a sub-index of the EMBI.

only counts the emblematic Chilean jaguar as a member. As is underscored by the decoupling of its risk premium from those of its Latin American neighbors, Mexico is increasingly regarded as an economy that is less aligned with other Latin American countries. The Mexican risk-premium spreads went from over 500 basis points higher than those attached to obligations of the US Treasury bonds to less than 150 basis points higher by mid 2005.[2] When the shocks to the Brazilian economy in 2002 took place, Mexico's risk premiums barely moved, an indication of Mexican solidity.

In reality, Mexico's affirmation by the financial markets also derived from an unprecedented macroeconomic transformation. During the 1990s Mexico experienced

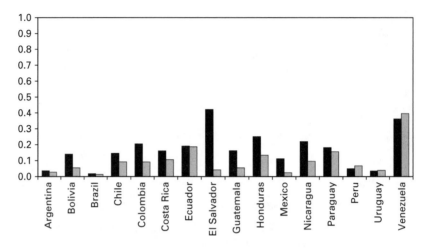

Figure 6.3
Herfindahl-Hirschman index of exports by types of products. Black
bars: 1986–1988. Gray bars: 1999–2001. Source: ECLAC.

deep economic changes. NAFTA, which went into effect
in 1994, tied Mexico to the United States, granting it an
anchor of exogenous credibility similar to what Spain
gained with its link to the European Union. The most visible part of this transformation was commercial, since the
economy experienced an unprecedented increase in its
non-oil exports. In a few years, Mexico went from being
a classic oil-exporting economy to becoming one of the
largest exporters of manufactured products in the world.
At the beginning of the 1980s, oil exports represented
more than two-thirds of Mexico's exports; in 2005, slightly more than one-tenth.

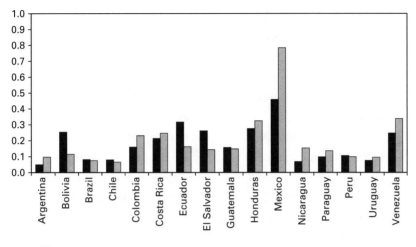

Figure 6.4
Herfindahl-Hirschman index of exports by countries of destination.
Black bars: 1986–1988. Source: ECLAC.

In the meantime, Mexico's exports of manufactured products experienced gigantic growth. According to the estimates of José Antonio Ocampo, Mexican exports of manufactured products of medium or high technology, meaning goods with significant added value, reached nearly 55 percent of the nation's total exports in 2000. To put this into perspective, for Chile, the regional economic champion, these kinds of exports barely represented 6.5 percent. The degree of opening of the Mexican economy, calculated by the income from imports added to the income from exports as a percentage of GDP, went from 27 percent in 1994 to more than 60 percent in 2004. The economy, too, became more competitive, increasing its participation in world trade. In 1984, Mexican exports represented 1.4 percent of the world's exports. Twenty years later, they exceed 2.6 percent of the world's exports.

Mexico's commercial transformation is unprecedented in Latin America. It exceeds even that of Chile, the regional champion with respect to dynamism and participation in international trade, if we take into account that the amount of Chile's exports of raw material is clearly superior to that of Mexico. This differential is evident in figures 6.3 and 6.4. The Herfindahl-Hirschman (HH) that measures the concentration or dispersion of exports by products and by countries, with 1 representing maximum concentration and 0 representing maximum diversification. As the figures show, the region continues to be highly dependent on the exporting of raw materials, such as oil, copper, gold, iron, nickel, coffee, and soybeans. (In 2005 these materials accounted for one-third of the region's exports, but more than 80 percent of Venezuela's, 70 percent of Peru's, and 60 percent of Chile's). Many Latin American countries continue to depend on the exporting of certain raw materials, Mexico being the great exception. In the periods 1986–1988 and 1999–2001, the proportion of raw materials in the region's total trade, while falling from 74 percent to 45 percent, continued to be high. The recent increase in demand from China, which benefits the soybean-exporting countries Argentina and Brazil and the copper-exporting countries Chile and Peru, may maintain or increase this dependence. The relatively reduced dependence on the exporting of raw materials has been accompanied by an increase in the exporting of manufactured products from 26 percent to 55 percent during the periods mentioned above. But this accomplishment is explained, to a great extent, by the Mexican trajectory, which displays one of the lowest dependency indexes on one or more exported products in the region, with a notable reduction in concentration by product in its exports. In other words, Mexico's good performance has skewed the overall results for Latin America. Most of the region's countries need to diversify their export base further.

Figure 6.4 points to one of Latin America's relative weaknesses (or strengths, depending on its neighbor's business cycle). It indicates a strong geographic dependence on Mexican exports. The United States effectively absorbs nearly 85 percent of Mexico's exports. This geographic dependence peaked during the periods 1986–1988 and 1999–2001, when the HH country index increased significantly, from 0.45 to 0.78.

This broad transformation of Mexico's production and export capabilities significantly reduced the volatility of its exports and its tax revenues. Calculated as a standard deviation, this volatility went from over 16 percent in 1984–1993 to 7 percent in 1994–2004. Parallel to this reduction in the volatility of its export income, Mexico's tax base, until then fundamentally dependent on oil and therefore on relatively volatile world prices, stabilized. Income gains derived from oil exports did not represent more than one-third of Mexico's fiscal receipts. One of Mexico's future challenges is how to increase its tax revenues, since tax collection does not exceed 15 percent of GDP (only about half the percentage in Turkey, and far from Brazil's rate of more than 35 percent). Even so, Mexico has been praised by the international community for enacting a remarkably rigorous economic policy, drastically reducing its budget deficit, and gaining control over government expenditures.

This first anchor—endogenous macroeconomic credibility with respect to its fiscal policies—has been accompanied by a second anchor with regard to monetary policy. Guillermo Ortiz, as head of the central bank of Mexico, enacted monetary policies that reduced inflation by nearly 15 percent between 1998 and 2002. The implementation of an inflation-targeting system with an explicit goal of 3 percent annual inflation, accompanied by a margin of about 1 percent, has allowed Mexico to achieve inflationary convergence with the United States. These stated goals were attained between 1999 and 2001, exceeded slightly in 2002, and sustained again in 2003, when Mexico's average inflation rate stabilized near 4.6 percent. (In 2004 it reached 5.2 percent, but in 2005 it went down to about 4 percent.) In tandem with this monetary stability, one can also observe institutional advances, with greater central bank independence. It is important to point out that Mexican authorities were able to decouple the timing of the presidential elections from that of the appointing of a governor for the central bank.

In achieving this separation of the timing of presidential terms and stewardship of its central bank, Mexico acquired one more institutional anchor.

Of course Mexico suffers from important ills related to disparities in income, to poverty, and to failures in tax collection, as do all countries. The less attractive face of the Mexican miracle continues to be the social aspect, the absence of investment addressing needs in education and health. This challenge will have to be addressed by improving the tax-collection system so that it will be possible to increase spending on second-generation social reforms. It is true that Mexico's proximity to the United States continues to be a decisive advantage ensuring its economic development, confirmed by Mexico's increasingly synchronization since 1994 with the US business cycle, just as Spain's economic takeoff in the 1980s was promoted by the European dynamic. Mexico also benefits from a top-quality anchor of exogenous credibility. As happened in Spain in 1959, Mexico in 1982 experienced a serious crisis that forced the authorities to begin a process of gradual reforms. In both cases, the crises and gradual trade opening were followed, at a distance of 20 years, by political transition, in 1975–1977 in the case of Spain and in 1997–2000 in the case of Mexico. In both countries the international links, via Europe for Spain in 1986, via the United States for Mexico in 1994, were decisive.

Its dependence on the United States certainly exposes the Mexican economy to the counter-shocks of the American business cycle, but a link of this type also constitutes an unequaled opportunity. Mexico is the only developing country that borders the world's most important economy. This border is a magnet, because the United States attracts Mexico's products as well as its citizens, and with these "exports" Mexico's entire GDP is pushed higher. It is also a guarantee, because Mexico's link to the United States functions as an insurance against all risks, as illustrated by the 1994 Tequila Crisis bailout.

But these ties between Mexico and the United States go beyond simple economic and financial connections. They extend into the social, political, cultural, and institutional realms. NAFTA prompted a fine institutional rain to fall over Mexico, since the country adjusted its accounting and judicial norms to the standards of its neighbor. The millions of Mexican immigrants who live in the United States send home funds that compare to direct foreign investment by the multinationals, at a pace equivalent to $1 billion per month (more than $16.5 billion in 2004, that is an amount equivalent to the total foreign direct investment received that year by Mexico), a fine rain that permeates the entire Mexican social fabric. In the United States, the Mexican immigrants' economic and political weight increases year after year, as shown by the American presidential elections and regional elections and in particular the recent elections of Antonio Villarraigosa as mayor of Los Angeles and Ken Salazar as one of Colorado's two U.S. senators. Bonds are woven on both sides that go beyond cold economic statistics and permeate the entire social and cultural fabric.

In a leisurely, pragmatic way, Mexico has combined its economic opening and policies with the State's control over the country's oil and the principal sources of energy. With some sound arguments, Mexico's main investors, including investment banks and companies with assets in the country, have been concerned about the possible election of the mayor of Mexico City, Andrés Manuel López Obrador, to the Mexican presidency in July 2006. However, what likely would follow would be more economic pragmatism. Both national and international institutions in fact reduce the possibility of any major policy shift away from the possibilist approach of the previous years.

From an international point of view, NAFTA has proven to be more powerful than a free-trade agreement tying three economies together. It works as a powerful institutional anchor. But Mexico also now counts on a wide range of national institutional stabilizers. Economic pragmatism and monetary and fiscal orthodoxy became the alphabet of nearly all politicians. In 2005 Manuel López Obrador tried to improve his image abroad by embarking on a market-friendly regional tour that included stops in Chile, in Brazil, and in the United States (including a visit to Wall Street). In the economic arena, the independence of the Banco Central de México is reflected not only in orthodox monetary policy but also in the institutional decoupling from the political cycle: the term of the Governor does not coincide with that of the president. No matter who becomes president in 2006, the governor can remain in office until 2009.

In the political field, the creation of the Instituto
Federal Electoral (IFE) is another relevant institutional
innovation. It allows independent supervision of democratic elections, consolidating the democratic dream of
Madero. After the achievement of investment-grade
status, as well as the stabilization of the macroeconomic
variables, the reduction in foreign debt and inflation, and
fiscal balance and a flexible-exchange-rate regime, there
are now these institutional stanchions in the shape of the
central bank and the IFE.

Mexico is building an unprecedented trajectory of
gradual advances, made by successive touches that are
far removed from its past revolutionary impulses and
any ideological extremes. The great difference between
Mexico and Chile or Brazil is that this process takes place
in the shadow of the United States. Mexico, like no other
Latin American country, benefits from an ace in its possibilist game. It follows in Chile's footsteps by avoiding
major mistakes that might deprive it of the precious
international investment grade consolidated in the period 1993–2006. Mexico, with 6 years of uninterrupted top
bond rating, now has joined the race for sustainable
development. Mexico's leaders know that such a qualifi-
cation can be lost (as happened with Colombia, which
benefited from an investment-grade rating for 6 years
before losing it). One can bet, however, that with its
anchors of endogenous and exogenous credibility,
Mexico will no longer deviate from its current trajectory
and will continue to set sail far from the shoals of the
political economy of the impossible.

7   The Emergence of
       a Political Economy
       of the Possible

We have learned that in order to treat the multiple problems and complexities of development we should elaborate generalizations in all kinds of fields, and not listen, like Ulysses, to the seductive song of the single paradigm.

—Albert Hirschman

The "possibilism" radiating from the experiences of Chile, Brazil, and Mexico amounts to another focus on political economy whose essence, in Hirschman's own words, "consists in figuring out avenues of escape from such straitjacketing constructs in any individual case that comes up."[1] The use of the term "possibilism," does not mean, however, that Latin Americans subscribe to the ideas Hirschman developed. The majority of them are not familiar with his name, and even if they were, there is no reason to think that they would be inspired directly by his ideas. However, the label "possibilism" does allow us to conceptualize the change in course from an older political and economic practice centered on a "utopian" view of time granting more value to the future (or the past) to a newer practice more concerned with the present. In Latin America, the future has ceased to be the horizon viewed from the present. Instead, a new horizon has emerged, very different from a place in time meant for a final judgment that will be formulated on the basis of close adherence to a single paradigm or to rigid imported models.

The fundamental evolution of the past two decades is, as Hirschman wrote, the move from "total confidence in the existence of a fundamental solution for social and economic problems to a more questioning, pragmatic attitude—from ideological certainty to more open-ended, eclectic, skeptical inquiry."[2] In the political realm, the democratization process has often been a product of pacts and agreements; that is, non-zero-sum cooperative games with mutual concessions and unrevealed preferences. The rhetoric of intransigence and ideological mistrust that prevailed during the military and authoritarian regimes have given way to the search for consensus and win-win negotiations in which opposition groups and political leaders compromise over principles and interests with the goal of preserving what is essential, to avoid the risk of being left out of the game and of not continuing to participate in the political process.

This aversion to ideological ardor, whether real or simulated, frames much contemporary Latin American discourse, and is apparent in the adoption of macroeconomic policies that show, as Hirschman underscores, "a new experimental spirit among Latin American economists,

intellectuals, and policy-makers."[3] Whether it is a matter
of the heterodox shocks in the struggle against inflation,
as in the case of the Austral and Cruzado plans implemented by Argentina and Brazil in the mid 1980s,
or the "social liberalism," "popular market economy," or
"growth with equity" policies acclaimed, respectively,
by Salinas in Mexico, Menem in Argentina, and Aylwin
and Frei in Chile during the 1990s, these examples illustrate the transformation of Latin America's political
economy toward more pragmatist formulas, the search
for an alchemy beyond any rigid paradigm. Instead of
wholly structuralist or monetarist solutions, purely neo-
liberal free-market, or idealistic social remedies, the preference now is for more flexible and nuanced economic
policies (that at times even combine economic liberalism
and political populism, as in the cases of Peru and
Argentina under Fujimori and Menem). Regarding privatization, meaning the realignment of the relationship
between the public and the private sector, whether the
retirement system or the opening to free trade, far from
fitting with all-or-nothing solutions, the policies enacted
display a degree of gradualism, with a clear preference
for enacting pragmatic reforms rather than definitive
ruptures.

   In an equally significant way, this change in world
view is apparent in the cognitive evolution of the UN's
Economic Commission for Latin America and the
Caribbean (ECLAC), whose reports have always
enjoyed considerable authority in the subcontinent. As

demonstrated by one of the first reports of the 1990s, the analytic focus shifted from the structural disadvantages inherited from the "lost decade" and sought to draw on the opportunities generated by policies learned by a "painful apprenticeship" and progress that had been made. So, in addition to the traditional, broad long-term planning perspectives, numerous case studies were undertaken that statistically converged to show certain successes in higher education, in the promotion of exports, and in industrial restructuring. As the report underlined, the fundamental focus rested on a new conviction that there are ways to overcome the severe obstacles faced by the region's countries. For ECLAC, which has a long tradition of somber analyses of the region's situation, this is, as Hirschman underscores, "a remarkable change and the promise of new openings."

Under the leadership of the Colombian José Antonio Ocampo, and now, of the Argentine José Luis Machinea, ECLAC's realignment has consolidated and accelerated. By mid 2005, the Santiago-based organization, once a leading light of heterodox economics, had organized a joint conference with the International Monetary Fund, a clear illustration of the new cognitive mood of constructive dialogue and pragmatist convergences between two leading international organizations that a few decades ago were regularly clashing in their respective views on the region.

The analytical reorientation to search for more constructive and pragmatic solutions has also been propelled

by other actors, including Guillermo Perry (the World
Bank's chief economist for Latin America), by the
Venezuelan Ricardo Hausmann (formerly chief economist at the Inter-American Development Bank, now a
professor at Harvard University), and later by the
Argentine Guillermo Calvo (the IADB's current chief
economist). All three of these men have worked in favor
of reasonable critiques of the market economy, denounc-
ing the sudden booms and busts that interrupt capital
flows that Calvo labeled "sudden stops" and Hausmann
called the "original sins" of economies incapable of yielding to the international financial markets when issuing
their own currency. This mismatch problem of countries
that can only issue debt in a foreign currency (mostly the
U.S. dollar) is at the heart of a recurring weakness in
Latin America's emerging economies, which financially
are tremendously open (i.e. dependent on foreign savings) and therefore exposed in their balance sheets to the
ebbs and flows of international finance and to exchange-
rate depreciations that directly affect their debt ratios.

Each of the above-mentioned leading economists has
made an effort to propose original solutions to ameliorate
the hardships of financial liberalization and to promote
better reforms with more emphasis on quality than on
quantity, particularly in creating and fostering institutions. They do not advocate either a drastic withdrawal
of the State from the economy or the State's omnipres-
ence in economics; they simply advocate finding a reasonable place for it within the market structure. The sole

forces and mechanics of the market are hardly perceived as the panaceas for all Latin American economic weaknesses.

In recent years these criticisms and proposals have become widely accepted and discussed in most economic circles. Prominent scholars (Barry Eichengreen at Berkeley, Andrés Velasco and Dani Rodrik at Harvard, Marc Flandreau at Sciences Po Paris), specialists in the financial industry (e.g. Avinash Persaud), and economists based at the University of Chicago, the alma matter of neo-liberalism (e.g. Luigi Zingales) have openly questioned the current financial globalization, situating it in a historical perspective and comparing it to the globalization of the 1890s or pointing out its limits and shortcomings. Their reflections echo a more general reconsideration shared by many economists in the United States who point to the chronic weaknesses of emerging market economies dependant on the U.S. dollar and exposed to the phenomena of debt intolerance that affects every country that has a long history of crises and debt defaults. These economists include former World Bank Chief Economist (and Nobel laureate) Joseph Stiglitz and former International Monetary Fund Chief Economist Kenneth Rogoff, who are both (from different perspectives) critical of dysfunctional capital markets.

Latin America's shift toward an emerging political economy of the possible is reaffirmed by the fact that some important political actors in countries as different as Mexico, Chile, and Brazil have approached this idea of the possible. The former Mexican president Carlos Salinas de Gortari, as well as the Minister of Finance under Patricio Aylwin, Alejandro Foxley, and Fernando Henrique Cardoso, elected senator a number of times and who served as Minister of Finance before becoming president of Brazil in October 1998, have all approached Hirschman's ideas, either close up or from afar—Salinas de Gortari because he studied with Hirschman at Harvard, Foxley because he benefited from Hirschman's support in creating one of the first think tanks sponsored by the Chilean opposition in the mid 1970s (CIEPLAN), and Cardoso because he is an assiduous reader of Hirschman's work. But many other prominent Latin American policy makers also shared Hirschman's passions and the interests, including the Brazilians who supported Cardoso (including Finance Minister Pedro Malan and José Serra, a likely candidate in Brazil's presidential election of 2006).

The intellectual and political trajectory of Fernando Henrique Cardoso also confirms that these conversions to the market and to a concept of democracy have more to do with life experiences than with theories, and that only with difficulty can they be reduced to a strict game of interest and convenience. As a sociologist Cardoso is known for his writings on development, which were aligned with the theory of dependence strongly inspired by Marxism and structuralism that prevailed in the ECLAC thinking of the 1950s and the 1960s. It was during this era that this son of a general and scion of a great

Brazilian family slipped away from Brazil's Communist
Party. From this point on, parallel to the arrival of the
military regime, Cardoso put aside his theoretical
approach to problematic issues, and democratization
became the essence of his work, to the detriment of
dependency theory. In 1975 he became actively committed to politics and was elected to the parliament. He was
reelected in 1982. Around that time, the references to
dependency theory, class struggle, and imperialist
exploitation dissipated with the mists of authoritarian
regimes. The ideas taken from Marxism vanished, and
new objects of interest appeared, such as entrepreneurship. Above all, the ideas of the Market and of
Democracy were seriously reevaluated and revalued.
During the 1980s, having experienced democracy as a
politician, Cardoso definitively abandoned the project of
a radical restructuring of society and embraced the
strategies of limited and bounded rationality.

**The Impossible Past and the Improbable Future:
Reconceiving the Past and Reconstructing the Future**

In Brazil, as in other places in the region, we have witnessed a considerable reemergence of rhetorical flexibility and of greater prudence, even reticence, when it comes
to applying predetermined models. To put it another
way, the good news from Latin America at the beginning
of the twenty-first century is that the region is on its way
to exorcizing a ghost that has long possessed it. This was

the ghost of a good theory that would solve all the problems and contribute to the laws of development, from which a simple and rational formula could be deduced that would be applicable from the Andes to Patagonia, as valid in Brazil as in Mexico.

Despite this remarkable evolution, the stereotypes and the frames of reference forged more than 20 years ago continue to survive. About 10 years ago, the insurrection in the southern Mexican state of Chiapas demonstrated how the rebel leader Subcomandante Marcos, whom *The Economist* called the Robin Hood of the Mayan jungle, could generate sympathy and resurrect the revolutionary archetypes hidden in memory. Suddenly, in the global time of market democracy, in the period of free trade and privatization amid which President Salinas dreamed of integrating Mexico with the implementation of NAFTA, Marcos, the Good Revolutionary, and his Zapatista guerrillas revived another time, that of revolutions and radiant futures that prevailed in the 1960s and the 1970s. With this Mexican episode, Latin America as a whole, as well as the Western world, witnessed a revolt in which issues involving the Third World, indigenous peoples, and revolutionary ideology joined forces yet again.

Although the Chiapas rebellion evinces a past that is still influential (and not only a mythic past, but also the real one of endemic misery affecting not only Chiapas but all Latin America), it also reveals the extent to which the conceptual and concrete universes of politics have been transformed. After the elections of August 1995,

Mexico chose the institutional path instead of that of
insurrection, and the arena of the voting booth tri-
umphed over the arena of the streets, furthering the
country's goal of democratization. This came to fruition
in July 2000 with the victory, for the first time in Mexican
history, of a presidential candidate from the opposition
party, Vicente Fox.

Yet Mexico's disenchantment with democracy coalesced in July 2003. After several years of sluggish economic growth, with the government trapped in internal
divisions and with Parliament increasingly paralyzed,
voters punished the National Action Party (PAN),
President Fox's political party. The number of PAN's
elected representatives sank from 207 to 153. This result
killed all possibilities for serious reforms in the second
half of Fox's presidential term, and the last attempt to
approve fiscal reform encountered internal divisions and
severe opposition in December 2003. The Mexican example illustrates the disadvantages of extreme possibilism
when pursued by governments with narrow margins for
parliamentary maneuvers and the inability to push forth
fiscal reforms or urgent measures in a country where tax
collection is limited and where the need for electricity,
infrastructure, education, and health services affects the
potential of an economy that borders the United States.

To a lesser degree, the Zapatista episode in Chiapas
corroborates the delay of economic reforms under Fox,
but also the piercing problem of the anti-military protests
in Chile and the civil and political reconversion of former

guerrilleros underway in Colombia, Ecuador, Peru, and Central America. Latin America as a whole finds itself at the crossroads of two time horizons: that of a past already proven impossible and that of a future which is still improbable. In fact, it seems that it is these two temporalities that hold sway over Latin America today.

Latin America's past is problematic. There is a wish to forget the face of the authoritarian regimes, the revolutionary violence, and the endemic miseries that particularly affect the indigenous populations (which one after the other have organized and have taken the reins of power, as shown by the rise of Alejandro Toledo in Peru and Evo Morales in Bolivia). Apart from joining the international financial world or accelerating the establishment of new industrial conquistadores, many Latin American countries have also turned to exploiting their natural resources in an effort to find a way out of the sinkhole of underdevelopment and thereby escape the past, hoping to partake in the global time of the First World.

However, the future remains as uncertain as it is problematic. What can be seen in Latin America today is precisely a crisis of the future, rather than an excess of "presentism." Political time horizons have become narrower, and countries have committed themselves to economic policies involving structural changes that are yet more adjustments involving time. These economic policies are more centered on the present than projected toward the future—in other words, economic policies are made with a view to more limited time horizons. What does this "tomorrow silence" mean for the political realm? The answer, far from inviting bewilderment, may instead tend to incite a greater optimism. As a matter of fact, the future that ended with the death of the great paradigms was accompanied by increasing skepticism regarding the siren song of political models proposing distant and infinitely better futures that depended upon the sacrifice of the present. The silence of the future, however disturbing it may be, cunningly conveys a positive element. With the narrowing of time horizons, one kind of world view disappears: that of great paradigms and infallible axioms designed to attain a golden age always announced for tomorrow (and postponed once tomorrow is attained). The downfall—or the asphyxiation—of teleological time, the emergence of a fragmented present, is accompanied not by the definitive closing of the future but by its opening to myriad possibilities. The future, liberated from the exhortations of History, transforms itself into an open time.

This devaluation of the future undeniably constitutes good news in a region accustomed to the promise of tomorrow, even if accompanied by difficulties. As shown by the policies of adjustment or of budgetary rigor, pragmatic experience has prevailed over eschatological expectations (of, for example, the advent of real democracy, or of the new man), which traditionally have pushed the future toward an ever more distant and fugitive tomorrow. In place of the golden age, past or yet to come, a time more urgently preoccupied with the present emerges: the time of budgetary equilibrium and controlled inflation—a time, in short, that wears down the eschatological expectations that make up a large part of Latin American history. In a continent born as a utopia—which is simultaneously a time that is not the present, and also one that is always yet to come—this shift constitutes important news. Today, the farthest horizons have ceased to be promising, or, at any rate, to be loaded with magical promises.

Nevertheless, the disappearance of the bright future creates difficulties. In politics, an offer is always articulated with respect to a future yet to be created. As Max Weber points out, "the politician is interested in the future and the responsibility toward the future."[4] The construction of the future—even with more limited horizons—constitutes one of the central dimensions of the political realm. To channel this future and articulate it, no longer as a fugitive agenda but in light of more defined and firm goals, appears to be among Latin America's current challenges. It is no longer a matter of reconceiving the past; it is now a matter of reconstructing a common future based on possibilities rather than on utopian enterprises.

The harmonization of political democracy, economic growth, and social equity is what is steering the arrow of Latin America at the present time. This arrow plots a trajectory to an "omnipresent present," as the Chilean sociologist Norbert Lechner puts it beautifully and accurately, where the past projects its shadow and the future its silences.

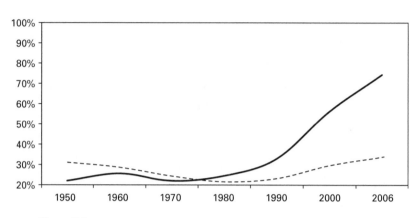

Figure 7.1
Increases in per-capita GDP (% with respect to world averages) of
China (—) and India (---). Based on data from Groningen Growth and
Development Centre, from Conference Board Total Economy
Database, and from BBVA forecasts.

The challenges ahead for Latin America's emerging
countries are not, as we see, exclusive to the region, but
neither are they impossible to face. It is true that difficulties abound and that in a quick historical retrospective
we can find strong arguments for pessimism. The intensive rounds of reforms of the past decade have failed to
take Latin America out of the trap of poverty and have
left a mix of successes and failures. Between 1990 and
2004, per-capita GDP rose less than 0.9 percent a year in
Latin America, while in the United States it rose 1.8
percent a year and in the world as a whole it rose 1.1 percent a year. Labor markets expelled workers from the
more protected formal sector to the informal one. The

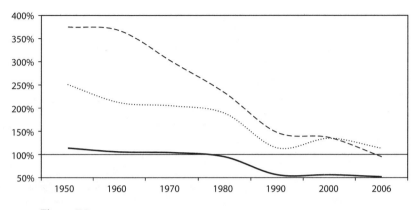

Figure 7.2
Decreases in per-capita GDP (% with respect to world averages) of
Venezuela (---), Argentina (···), and Peru (—) Based on data from
Groningen Growth and Development Centre, from Conference Board
Total Economy Database, and from BBVA forecasts.

gaps between high-income brackets and low-income
brackets did not decrease during the 1990s; they
increased.

However, if we take a longer perspective not all the
stories look the same. Some countries have behaved better than others in managing to curb the downward
trends. If we compare the evolution of per-capita GDP in
Latin American countries with that in the rest of the
world, we see that the region's emerging countries have
not caught up as much as India and China have.
Venezuela, Argentina, and Peru even experienced continuous slumps in per-capita GDP. But Chile and Mexico
managed to reverse the deterioration, and Brazil

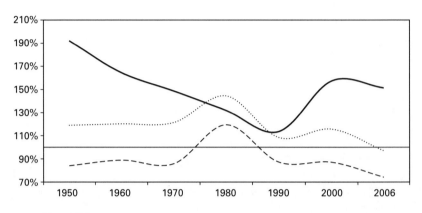

Figure 7.3
Evolution of per-capita GDP (% with respect to world averages) in
Mexico (···), Chile (—), and Brazil (---). Based on data from Groningen
Growth and Development Centre, from Conference Board Total
Economy Database, and from BBVA forecasts.

managed to smooth it. These are precisely the countries
in which a new cognitive style of political economy
emerged.

The time of a supposed end of history and of the bright
and sunny future, with a naive interpretation of a unique
road to development, seems to have passed in many
countries of the region. Good Revolutionaries and
Market Fundamentalists, equally loaded with ideolo-
gism and maximalism, depicting realities in black and
white rather than in *clair-obscurs*, seem to have
retrenched. In Chile, in Brazil, and in Mexico, reforms
have been infused with pragmatism. Policy makers have
adapted reforms to local capacities and realities.

Significant progress has been attained. There is a generalized recognition by policy makers of the need to achieve and preserve macroeconomic balances. The days of hyperinflation are over, and in many countries, while the population's tolerance for high prices has diminished, inflation has been reduced to below one-digit rates. Fiscal deficits have been contained. Chile is even enjoying impressive fiscal surpluses. In other nations, once-closed economies have begun to expand their exports rapidly and are diversifying in terms of items exported and markets of destination.

That does not mean, once again, that history is over: this transformation is an unfinished journey, and it might be reversed. In some countries Good Revolutionaries and Free Marketeers are still alive. Yet what is also striking is that they tend to wear the habits of the time, their anti-market rhetoric contrasting with their pragmatic management of the economy.

As we will see in the next chapter, from Caracas to Buenos Aires, Latin America is not out of the woods of utopianism, and the seduction of the political economy of the impossible still lives on. Still, the new masters of the Venezuela's Bolivarian free-market counter-revolution seem to differ in their policy-making style from the neo-Keynesian policy makers of Mar del Plata. Once again, Latin America invites a pluralistic vision and nuances, in a region where open and conflicting possibilities abound.

8   Argentina and Venezuela: Enduring Neo-Populism

Beyond the difficulties associated with Latin America's vanishing horizon of infinite promises, it is necessary to pay attention to the multiplicity of the region's trajectories and paradoxes. In many of these countries, the emergence of possibilism reveals itself as having multiple forms, but it often exhibits a singular populist habit.

In Peru, in Argentina, and in Venezuela, the 1990s were characterized by the return of relatively charismatic and effusive leaders who evoked contradictory feelings in their call to the people, from the dispossessed to the landless waiting for Godot to liberate them from a time without horizons. These same leaders became masters of the great big change. Once elected, some implemented broad free-market therapies, illustrating in this way the Latin American pragmatism evident at the end of the twentieth century. This electoral calculus gave way to a policy of reforms. Once the populist velvet glove was cast off, a formidable neo-liberal iron fist was revealed. The neo-populist experiences can also be seen as the inevitable subversion of the great Latin American transformation.

Whether we speak of Carlos Menem in Argentina, Alberto Fujimori in Peru, or Hugo Banzer in Bolivia, the sequence, with some minor variations, turns out to be the same: anti-establishment and anti-free-market election campaigns, then an about-face and the implementation, often at high speed, of a series of liberal free-market reforms that make any monetarist initiatives pale by comparison. Once the population has swallowed the bitter pill of free-market reforms, what is essential for the tightrope-walking neo-populist leader is that he maintain his equilibrium in the polls (and, sometimes, arrange for his re-election). Put another way, his essential line of conduct is to call on the people and give himself over to them, attempting to satisfy their expectations for the longest possible time, but always arranging short-term tactics with longer-term strategies. From the tension between these two temporalities a particularly pragmatic management style emerges, one that is opportunistic and zigzags between a populist economic policy platform (promising immediate and painless redistribution policies) and anti-populist policies (to spread the cost of reforms among the different opposing groups). In all these cases, neo-liberalism has been instituted by surprise.

Halfway between the democratic pro-tempore form of government, always fitting within predefined temporal limits, and the authoritarian government, which aspires only to distance itself from the temporal coercions of democratic life, the tightrope-walking neo-populist operates in a temporal interval. Menem and Fujimori both practiced the art of postponement, despite knowing that they could not do so indefinitely. These leaders—at least in the case of Menem—did not question the essence of their democratic regimes and kept on playing the rules of the game. Regarding economic matters, they did not reject the rules governing the market. They played in two different temporal registers: a short-term one (in which the goal was to force-feed the pill of painful reforms by waving, as needed, the populist flag) and a longer-term one (that of re-election). As the studies that took place after these experiences underscore, these same leaders appeared to absorb a political lesson that distinguished them from their populist predecessors. Far from betting only on populist myopia (using a short-term strategy of income and tax redistribution to gain the population's support), they bet on structural adjustment, conscious of the foreseen short-term costs in unemployment and the negative effect on wages. They were also fully aware that populations cannot be completely fooled by intertemporal tradeoffs. The wage increases and relaxed budgetary policies of today do not announce a better tomorrow; they generate future tax increases, and, in the long, run, even more painful adjustments.

Argentina, or the Sirens' Song

Carlos Menem was not Juan Perón, nor is "menemismo" the same as "peronismo." The neo-liberal policies implemented under the menemist tango hardly fit with the

traditional pattern of peronismo. The fact is that
Argentina under Menem and his finance minister
Domingo Cavallo implemented one of the broadest
reforms experienced in the 1980s by a Latin American
country and made an entire country dance a furious neo-
liberal tango. They did not hesitate to abandon entire
aspects of monetary sovereignty when in 1991 they
implemented the Convertibility Law and pegged
Argentina's currency to the U.S. dollar at a one-to-one
conversion rate. This policy's goal was to stop hyperinflation and prevent the government from monetizing its
deficit, or, what amounts to the same thing, from abandoning itself to the macroeconomics of populism.
(Rudiger Dornbusch and Sebastián Edwards devoted an
entire book to describing these policies.) For a while, this
convertibility was very effective in forcing down the bitter pill of structural adjustment, while at the same time
acting the populist role (for internal purposes) and the
technocratic one (for external purposes). Yet this policy
ultimately resulted in a straitjacket, and in 1999 Menem
abandoned his hopes for reelection after his attempt to
run for a third term was ruled unconstitutional.

Besides acting to satisfy the Argentine electorate,
"menemismo" also tried to appeal to another type of
financially interested voter. Like other countries in the
region, Argentina has important needs with regard to
financing its current balance of payments, making it sensitive to international capital flows. Under Menem,
Argentina had to seduce international investors on a

large scale. With some slight exaggeration, one can speak of a two-faced populism: the tightrope-walking neo-populists and the neo-liberal free-marketeers are obliged to execute the difficult and delicate art of satisfying two partners at once. In January 1999, this game of trust and mistrust was embodied in the call to the international financial markets initiated by Menem at the time the Brazilian real was devalued. Then the Argentine president launched the campaign for dollarization, going a step beyond the Convertibility Law and essentially adopting the U.S. dollar as Argentina's de facto currency unit. The purpose behind this strategy was to alleviate the financial market's mistrust and to win over the business analysts and Wall Street investors who had been made uneasy by the Argentine economy's dependence on Brazil, which at the time absorbed 30 percent of Argentina's exports. Analysts at merchant banks and investment firms quickly altered their perceptions, convinced by the Argentine government (which increased its road shows in New York, Paris, and London) that Argentina was not vulnerable to the spillovers from Brazil.

The history of the post-Menem period showed the limits of these confidence games, and Menem's successor, Fernando De la Rúa, was unable to escape financial dependence. The 1990s led Argentina to a dead end. The subsequent issuing of bonds to finance a country that was not able to raise taxes because of the economic slowdown, to curb tax evasion, or to contain its expenditures

resulted in one of the most spectacular debt defaults in
the history of emerging markets. Toward the end of 2001,
Argentina was forced to restructure its monumental debt.
As a consequence, the following year Argentina experienced one of the most severe recessions in its economic
history and a spectacular dive of its per-capita GDP. In
2002 its growth rate was –11 percent of GDP from the previous year, a drop not equaled since the beginning of the
twentieth century. The country experienced a vertiginous
fall in purchasing power abroad. Thousands of
Argentines fell into poverty. Bank runs and street
protests amplified the crisis. The Argentine crisis was felt
even in Europe, where businesses exposed in Latin
America, especially Spanish firms, felt the hit and were
punished in the stock market. More that 500,000 holders
of Argentine bonds, especially in Italy and Germany,
mobilized against the Argentine State by creating bond-
holders' committees in order to try to recover some of the
value of their investments. The inauguration of a new
president, Néstor Kirchner, marked a rallying point. The
rhetoric of the new president, combined with the more
interventionist economic policies of his Minister of
Finance, Roberto Lavagna, restored, for a time, the government's popularity and its ability to direct a country
that had lost its economic compass after the declaration
of a suspension of payments.

The history of Argentina's recovery from the crisis is
far from over. In 2004 and 2005 the country once again

achieved a high rate of economic growth and had inflation under control. In 2005 it restructured its defaulted
debt and maintained growth while keeping inflation
under control. Whatever the final outcome, Argentina's
trajectory in the 1990s and the 2000s is proof that the
search for economic shortcuts is fatal and that no miracle
recipes exist. Lasting growth cannot be achieved without
macroeconomic stability, which becomes impossible
when there is too great a flight of capital. Argentina's trajectory will also remain a stigma for all purists and
absolute defenders of "chemically pure" free-market
elixirs.

In the 1990s, when its free-market miracle was at the
top of the indexes charting structural reforms, Argentina
was treated to an avalanche of praise from the
International Monetary Fund and the World Bank. Today,
a more cautious enthusiasm emanates from multilateral
institutions when they consider Argentina's experience.
In Argentina the road ahead also seems much more sus-
picious of Grand Theory schemes, even if a more populist style predominates. In spite of its less market-friendly approach, the Kirchner administration rejected re-
nationalization of privatized utilities and 1970s-style
populist policies, but Kirchner's government ruled out
any return to the neo-liberal policies pursued by
Argentina in the 1990s.

Some argue that the neo-liberal formulas were poorly
applied, that privatizations took place inadequately, and

that Argentina's economic, legal, and political institutions were too fragile. No doubt one of the greatest lessons to be learned from Argentina derives from the institutional imperative: as "mea culpa" reports from UN agencies and from many academics (in line with Douglass North) now insist, institutional maturity is one of the fundamentals of economic stability.

The pendulum of reforms seems to have reached an equilibrium where the State occupies a higher profile. Ultimately, behind the institutions hides the famous concept of governance, meaning the capability or incapability to govern, to establish stable norms and institutions. Recent work by Daron Acemoglu and by Stephen Haber only deepens this evidence and intensifies the analytical path tinged with possibilism. One of the difficulties inherent in consolidating institutional reforms is the temporal dynamic. "First-generation" reforms (privatizations, deregulations, liberalizations, and so on), though politically powerful in the short term, are not consolidated without "second-generation" reforms oriented toward education and health care, or infrastructures and judicial institutions, interwoven economically and legally, whose beneficial effects are not reaped until years later, as they are limited to brief electoral mandates. This is often too late for the leaders who implemented the reforms to harvest the political dividends of their political courage. This temporal coercion is, without doubt, one of the great challenges facing Latin America in this decade.

Hugo Chávez

Populist rhetoric is also omnipresent in Venezuela, but the situation President Hugo Chávez faces is not similar to that faced by Argentina's president at the beginning of the 1990.

When Carlos Menem, the candidate of Argentina's Justicialista party, acceded to the presidency in 1989, he inherited a slightly crazy economy, as Chávez did 10 years later in Venezuela, only to a different degree. Argentina, unlike Venezuela, suffered from a macroeconomic shock of great magnitude. Hyperinflation—which reached 3,000 percent in 1989—provoked a drastic contraction of investment and growth. Subjected to extreme variations in the inflation rate, Argentines experienced a remarkable narrowing of their temporal horizons. Since 1985, the maximum duration of loan operations did not exceed 7 days, in contrast to 90 days in a normal period. Beginning with this hyperinflationary shock, all attempts to make projections or to form projects were fraught with obstacles. The country was mature enough to face any therapy, even shock therapy, capable of breaking the inflationary spiral. The temporal shock of hyperinflation was followed by its necessary remedy: structural adjustment and the imposition of convertibility. Pegging the peso to the dollar, and thereby anchoring monetary policy in a radical way, was the ultimate weapon against spiraling inflation. Controversial privatization of utilities (including oil companies, the post office, and electrical

and water utilities) and a massive influx of foreign direct
investment helped to fix the budgets and tame inflation
(from 5,000 percent a year in the late 1980s to virtually
zero in the early 1990s) and to improve the economy, but
at the cost of considerable unemployment. With the help
of this neo-liberal shock therapy, implemented as a quick
fix, the pendulum of Argentina's economy returned to its
normal rhythm. The two remedies were supported by a
forward-looking consensus. The legitimacy of the correc-
tive action taken was grounded not so much in improbable future expectations of the effectiveness of these
reforms as in Argentineans' profound desire to escape
the hyperinflation then present.

    In Venezuela, in spite of the severe economic crisis
affecting the country by the end of 1990s, there was no
such temporal shock. The fundamental difference
between the two economies is due to the variable of oil.
In no other country in Latin America has income from oil
exports been such a blessing and a curse. It has made
Venezuela rich, but it has also exposed it to the uncertain-
ty of the oil markets. Remember that the Venezuelan
economy's dependence on oil increased, even under
Chávez, with respect to previous years. Hydrocarbons
made up nearly 85 percent of Venezuelan exports in 2004
(in contrast to 70 percent in 1999), 30 percent of GDP (versus 25 percent in 1999), and approximately 55 percent of
tax revenues (versus 38 percent in 1999). In fact, the
Venezuelan economy experiences periodic "accordion
hits" in resonance with oil booms and busts: each dollar

lost or earned translates into a loss or a gain of a billion dollars in exports; that is, slightly more than 1 percent of GDP, for a contraction in tax revenue of nearly 0.5 percent of GDP.

Such variable income confers, nevertheless, a certain security with regard to the future of Venezuelan leaders. It confers a temporal horizon longer than that faced by Argentina's policy makers. In Venezuela, policies are based less on a rejection of a painful past than on fanning promises of a radiant future with the hope for a return to the golden age that the Venezuelans knew during the oil boom that transformed the economy in an ephemeral moment of magical realism. With the oil boom off the mid 1970s, enormous wealth poured into the country, but the vast lower class benefited little. Oil prices dropped in the late 1980s, and once again the country was thrown into crisis. In 1983, as oil prices declined and debt spiraled, the bolívar was devalued. Since then, Venezuela has grown steadily poorer. By 1990, riots had swept through Caracas and had been violently repressed. Two coup attempts took place in 1992. However, with oil prices recovering, the good old days of shining temporal horizons came back during the 2000s. Venezuela is brimming with oil, and the estimated life of its reserves is longer than 60 years at the current pace of extraction. Its situation looked very different from that of Argentina in 2000.

With such a long temporal horizon, it is difficult for Venezuelan leaders to implement drastic reforms or

structural adjustments, which are politically and economically costly in the short-to-medium term. In the case
of Chávez, the rhetoric of promises is only reaffirmed by
the recovery of oil prices, consolidated between 2002 and
2006, a recovery that not only put the economy at ease
but also kept the specter of unpopular measures at bay.

The sources of support and of fragility underlying
chavismo are very different from those of menemismo.
Undeniably, Chávez shares with Argentina's leader a
similar desire to accelerate the rhythm of his country's
economic transformation, using the entire arsenal of ref-
erenda (six polls in the years 1999 and 2000). For example, the initial 6-month time limit on the drafting of a new
constitution was reduced to a few weeks. But will
Chávez, like Menem, decide to alter the promises made
during an election and avoid washing up on the shoals of
a populist macroeconomy?

Verbal jousts and confrontational posturing have esca-
lated and have radicalized an opposition bound together
only by its rejection of a democratically elected populist
president. This is an opposition that depleted, in record
time, the essence of its political capital. In 2002, with the
conflict for the political control of PVDVA (the state-
owned oil company) widening and with street protests
proliferating, Venezuela's political crisis became more
intense. The country abandoned controlled exchange
rates and opted for floating the currency in February in
order to let market forces determine the value of the
money. A year later, however, to limit depreciation but

also to curb capital flight and ensure more control of the private sector, Chávez endorsed the interventionist option and reinstated exchange-rate controls. In December 2002 he was trapped by a general strike that extended to the oil industry and paralyzed the country. The case of Venezuela demonstrates the tenacity of the utopian habits in Latin America, with both the government and the opposition intensifying confrontation and rhetorical intransigence. President Chávez was still playing the double game of seduction at which Menem became a master: he worked to satisfy his fellow citizens while, at the same time, not upsetting foreign investors too much. The vocabulary of the Chavist revolution was therefore also reflected in a high-tech discourse designed to seduce foreign investors, or at least to attempt to halt their flight. Capital flight was indeed practiced enthusiastically by wealthy Venezuelans, whose current capital held abroad is estimated at over $20 billion (equal to one-fifth of Venezuela's GDP). To judge by the reactions of the financial analysts and the rating agencies, however, this attempted seduction, aimed at winning financial votes, turned out to be less successful than one by the Argentine government. Moody's Investors Service, not carried away by enthusiasm for Chávez during his campaign or after his election in December 1998, lowered its investment ratings for Venezuela twice in 1998, once in July and once in September.

After the attempted coup d'état of April 2002, the response of the markets approached euphoria. This coup

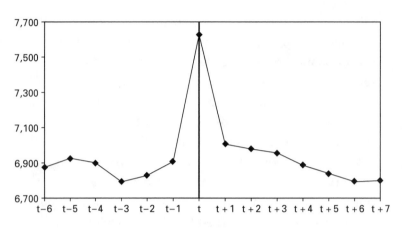

Figure 8.1
Index of the Caracas Stock Exchange around the time of the attempted coup against Chávez (represented by the vertical line at t). Source: BBVA Provincial, 2005.

was interpreted as an attempt to throw out a leader who was not very friendly to the market. The more liquid stocks traded on the Caracas Exchange reached record levels, and the index grew by nearly 1,000 points in a single trading session when it appeared that Chávez had been deposed. When in the following days it became apparent that the coup had failed, the index fell again. The spreads, too, reflected this enthusiasm, dropping nearly 200 basis points, in order to adjust to the rise the market would experience as soon as Chávez's return to power was made known. Since the end of 2003, the Venezuelan spread—that is, the premiums required by foreign investors—stayed particularly low, partly as a

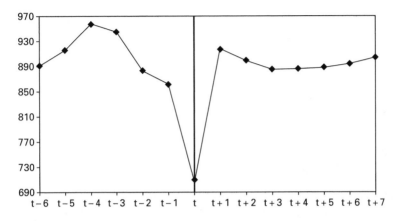

Figure 8.2
Spread EMBI+ for Venezuela around the time of the attempted coup against Chávez (represented by the vertical line at t). Source: BBVA Provincial, 2005.

result of the increasing price of oil and partly because an excess of international liquidity turned toward emerging countries in search of profits.

The Chávez experience was resolved with a spectacular contraction of Venezuela's per-capita income in 2002 and 2003 (–9 percent for these two years), a decline not experienced since the 1930s. This was accompanied by a sudden rise in unemployment, as 18 percent of the active working population was officially unemployed in 2003. Well-off Venezuelans cast a no-confidence vote, judging by the massive capital flight which took place between 1999 and 2003, which amounted to over $35 billion. Capital flight represented more than 5 percent of

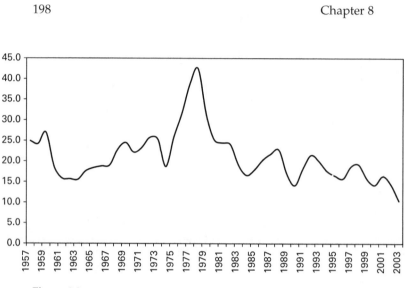

Figure 8.3
Investment in Venezuela (total investment, in % of GDP), 1957–2004.
Source: BBVA Continental, 2005.

Venezuela's GDP before Chávez became president. Capital flight rates increased in the aftermath of his inauguration, and doubled at the beginning of 2000, reaching nearly 12 percent of GDP. The examination of investment levels alone illustrates the degree to which the current problems of the Venezuelan economy have distant roots in the past. As figure 8.3 shows, a declining ratio of investment, public and private, is not new in Venezuela. This decline points to a continual loss of confidence in the economy since the end of the 1970s. In other words, Chávez did not invent the crisis but rather amplified and magnified it. After he came into power, the downward trend of investment continued, as if he was pursuing the destructive heritage of his predecessors who were unable to curb this loss of confidence.

Other data confirm that, rather than inventing a crisis, Chávez is amplifying one. After the end of the world oil crisis of the early 1970s, the purchasing power of Venezuelans eroded. Venezuela was prosperous between 1960 and 1980 (with an average growth rate close to 5.5 percent, one of the highest in the region), but it has suffered nine recessions since 1975. Venezuela's economic growth stagnated, remaining at just at 0.25 percent of annual GDP growth between 1980 and 2002. During this period, per-capita income sank back to the levels experienced in the 1940s. During the period 1980–2005, while the population increased by 2.7 percent, the average annual growth rate of GDP was 0.8 percent. In 1965, per-capita income was 120 percent higher than in other developing countries and was close to 500 percent of the per-capita income of countries in Southeast Asia. In 2000, Venezuela's GDP represented no more than 40 percent of the average income among developed countries and averaged less than 75 percent of the income in Southeast Asian countries. Productivity among Venezuelan workers in the non-oil sector has declined by 50 percent since 1980. Echoing this macroeconomic volatility is a political volatility characterized by an increasing rate of turnover among elected officials. Venezuela's parliamentary volatility was one of the lowest in Latin America during the 1980s, with an annual average of 15 percent. During the 1990s, along with Peru, it reached 40 percent, the highest

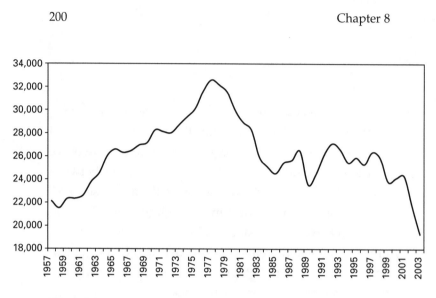

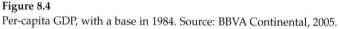

Figure 8.4
Per-capita GDP, with a base in 1984. Source: BBVA Continental, 2005.

figures for the region during this decade. In other words, the economic decline was not just vertiginous, but it also preceded Chávez's accession to power: Chávez did not invent the crisis; he inherited it and made its own contribution to amplify it.

Once he acquired control of oil, Chávez began to deepen Venezuela's "Bolivarian Revolution." In his speeches, utopian and socialist accents became omnipresent, reviving the good old days of Good Revolutionaries. "Savage neo-liberalism" and globalization became the usual suspects of poverty and corruption in the country. Unlike his Brazilian socialist neighbor, Chávez moved away from possibilism, leaving aside fiscal prudence with the help of the oil boom and non-

interventionist policies. In 2004 the economy bounced
back from the strike with the growth momentum fueled
by high oil prices and massive spending by the central
government, which rose from 19 percent of the GDP in
1999, when Chávez arrived, to more than 31 percent of
GDP in 2004. Even with massive tax receipts, pushed by
oil prices, the government's fiscal deficit reached 2.8 percent in 2004, and public debt rose from less than 30 percent of the GDP in 1999 to 40 percent.

By 2005, while oil prices keep skyrocketing, the ever-
extending tentacles of Chávez's "21st-century socialism"
reached nearly all the parts of the economy. Private enterprise and property rights are theoretically guaranteed by
the 1999 constitution that Chávez himself fathered before
he much more openly embraced socialism. New types of
businesses dubbed "social production companies" prolif-
erate, most of them closely tied to the hands of the State,
while co-operatives and co-management increase.
Expropriations of firms and of land also were on the rise.
In 2003, the government launched agro-industrial businesses in order to supply staples such as milk and maize
at low prices, and it created a retail food chain in order to
supply basic food products. (Since then, Mercal has
grabbed 40 percent of the market for staple foodstuffs.)
After the August 2004 referendum, Chávez extended the
visible hand of the State over many other segments of the
economy. He set up a new state airline, a cement firm and
a phone company. Banks have been ordered to earmark,
at subsidized rates, nearly 30 percent of their total loans

for housing and farming. In 2005, the bankrupt paper
firm Venepapel (now Invepal) was confiscated and then
put back in operation under a co-management scheme.
With the exchange-rate controls retained, and with price
limits and credit regulations increased, the government
achieved a stranglehold not only on political institutions
but also on economic institutions.

Venezuela's economy is more and more under government control, in line with its increasing political power.
Since late 1998, when he was first elected president,
Hugo Chávez has achieved sweeping victories and
defeated the opposition in nine votes, including a parliamentary poll in December 2005. He has survived an
attempted coup d'état that briefly ousted him and a
strike-cum-lockout that paralyzed the entire economy.
Both events reinforced his image of a "democrat" fighting against adverse winds. In August 2004, he called a
referendum on his presidency and won in spite of the
fraud protests of the opposition. Two months later the
same opposition lost key support in local government,
leaving only two of the 23 country's states out of the control of Chávez's allies.

The outcome of all these political fights, street mobi-
lizations, oil strikes, failed coup d'état and elections, is
that nowadays Chávez enjoys untrammeled power while
his presidential popularity rating soared to 70 percent in
opinion polls. His control over all political institutions of
the state is complete. Besides running the executive
branch and consolidating its control over the parliament,

in December 2004 he clinched control of the judiciary with the nomination of 12 extra pro-government judges to the Supreme Court to replaced disloyal ones.

The poorest Venezuelans see Chávez as their champion in a failing country, while members of the country's fast-shrinking middle class perceive him as a more sinister figure. The latter accuse him of perverting democracy with authoritarian accents and taking a market economy into a neo-communist utopian dream (or nightmare). But with Venezuela's oil wealth, Chávez has a powerful way to provide food, schools, and doctors[1] to the poor. The results of these massive social policies are mixed, however. Rather than decreasing, poverty is rising. In 1999, 54 percent of households were poor; in 2004, according to official figures, the percentage exceeded 60.

Not only is the political economy of the impossible alive in Venezuela; it may also reach other countries. Chávez's utopian style might look tropical to many other Latin American governments, but the color of oil is much more appealing to them. Chávez's "petro-diplomacy" is very active around the region and is obliging the United States to look at Latin America more carefully. In 2005 Chávez launched Telesur, a new pan-American television station, with help from other Latin American governments (including Argentina, Cuba, and Uruguay) but with 70 percent of the financing coming from Caracas. This tropical CNN is not the sole initiative of a Bolivarian leader who used the oil windfall in order to spread the revolution or at least to counter the power of American "imperialism" in the region. Telesur comes on the heels of other initiatives looking to secure new friends in the region. In 2005, Venezuela bought more than US$900 million of Argentina's debt and a large amount of Ecuador's. By the middle of that year, Chávez had set up several oil initiatives, including Petrosur (with Argentina and Brazil), Petrocaribe (under which it is offering twelve Caribbean countries cheap credit for oil imports), and Petroandina (under which Chávez offered other Andean presidents co-operation on pipelines and refining). Chávez is also reviving Simon Bolívar's dream of continental integration, and he claims to be building an alternative (called ALBA) to the Free Trade Area of the Americas. And by the end of 2005 he had joined the Mercosur.

Happy to pocket Venezuelan subsidies, most of the neighbors only listen politely to Chávez. Only Cuba has signed on to the ALBA project, and most countries are unenthusiastic about Petrocaribe or figure that Petrosur and Petroandina feature much rhetoric and little action. It seems, however, that revolutionary echoes are still appealing in the region. Above all, the Venezuelan experience confirms that diversity still prevails in Latin America, and that old rhetoric and old policies survive and have been revived there.

Paradoxically, reformist progress has been relatively mild in Venezuela. This may turn into a blessing in disguise. Future post-Chavist leaders may take inspiration from past situations and capitalize on the potential of an economy that continues to be one of the greatest unrealized promises of Latin America. For example, take the case of the public oil enterprise PDVSA. If it were to be privatized, it would have a market value equal to twice Venezuela's GDP and nearly 10 times the value of Venezuela's external debt. The exceptional untapped potential of Venezuela is one of the highest in the region, as one can see by looking at Venezuela's economic history in the 1970s, when annual GDP growth exceeded 5 percent. By simultaneously increasing investment and productivity and by enacting economic reforms, Venezuela, with natural resources unequaled in the region, could find less volatile paths to growth.

What is remarkable in the political realm is that, regardless of the strong polarization and politicization of its society, Venezuela continues to bet on democracy. While Chávez and his followers celebrated their victory, Latinobarómetro published the results of a 2004 poll. Support for democracy turned out to be stronger in Venezuela than anywhere else in Latin America except Uruguay. Seventy-four percent of Venezuelans said they preferred democracy to any other form of government and 86 percent considered democracy to be the only political system likely to help the development of the country—a record percentage in Latin America. Pandora's box, opened by Chávez, has of course not been closed. But the country of the Good Revolutionary is also the country of the Good Democrat, with an extraordinarily vital civil society that is committed to democracy. It is

likely that Venezuelans will continue to be strong supporters of democracy, and that either in 2006 (the year of
the next presidential elections) or later the present government and the opposition will meet again in elections
in order to voice their disagreements in the voting booths
rather than on the streets.

Conclusion: The Hedgehog, the Fox, and the Chameleon

Better, surely, not to pretend to calculate the incalculable, not to pretend that there is an Archimedean point outside the world whence everything is measurable and alterable; better to use in each context the methods that seem to fit it best, that give the (pragmatically) best results; to resist the temptations of Procrustes. . . .

—Isaiah Berlin[1]

In one of his most famous essays, the English philosopher Isaiah Berlin proposed the distinction between two ideal types of human spirit. The "hedgehogs" are those who organize life and their thoughts in terms of a unique and self-referential world view. The "foxes" are those who chase down multiple tracks, pursuing various and strongly contradictory goals simultaneously, diverging here and there, always guided by a pluralist worldview.

The great Latin American economic and political transformation could well consist of this turn in spirit and a view of a world populated with more foxes than hedgehogs, a world where self-referential and monochromatic outlooks have been succeeded by more pluralistic and multicolored visions. This transformation may be transitory. As Isaiah Berlin explained, the ardent desire of foxes often consists of reaching that self-referential and monochromatic world vision. Possibilist democrats, sharing this more pluralistic and less holistic view of world affairs and policy issues, seem to have proliferated in the past two decades. This transformation, no doubt, is only partial, since many former hedgehogs, Marxists Good Revolutionaries or Neo-Liberal Free-Marketeers, pretend to have become foxes when all they have done is falsify their preferences, change them, or exchange one paradigm for another, the matrix being kept unchanged and still driven by the absolute law of an inflexible paradigm. The emergence of the political economy of the possible is, however, good news in a region affected by the neo-Marxist and neo-liberal ideologies of the twentieth century.

A Critical Juncture

In 2006, Latin America is again at a critical juncture. Some will celebrate the advances that have been achieved—in particular, the synchronized growth rates registered in three successive years (2004–2006), an achievement not heard of since the 1960s. Others will focus their attention on poverty and inequality, which are still holding back development in the region. However, beyond short-term data and achievements, the profound and subtle transformation taking place in Latin America—a transformation that stems from surging economic pragmatism—is worth celebrating.

When recent decades are put in perspective, what really stands out are the profound transformations that give rise to a "bias for hope" (as Albert Hirschman would say), in contrast with *fracasomanía* (failure syndrome). External factors—low interest rates, costly raw materials, and Asian growth—are lining up to boost Latin America's GDP. However, what draws the most attention is that since the 1980s Latin America has been searching for ways to grow through pragmatic economic policies. It is inventing and creating institutional masts, looking for monetary and fiscal anchors, and it is doing all of this outside the predetermined paths of any rigid ideological model.

The Chilean example is, from this point of view, exemplary and perhaps unique. In Chile the privatization of pension funds remained a regulatory jewel of top-quality institutional craftsmanship. Year after year, the system was modified and adjusted. Today the Chilean regulation body, the Superintendencia, is one of the most credible, technically prestigious, and highly esteemed institutions in the country.

This reform, above all, symbolizes the profound change that Chile underwent in the last two decades as it invented a pragmatic and gradual political economy after years of ideological tidal waves. In the 1970s, social and liberal revolutions occurred which were built up and thrown against countries, in both cases searching to implement rigid paradigms invented in other hemispheres. The Good Neo-Liberal was nothing more than another side to the Good Revolutionary, both of them coinciding in their search for impossible economic policies. In the 1980s and especially in the 1990s, economic pragmatism prevailed. With the return to democracy, there could have been a temptation to create yet another model and break with the previous regime. This was not the case, however. Chilean democrats decided to carry on with the reforms already underway by trying to combine monetary and fiscal orthodoxy with social reforms and balanced growth. After 1989, the year democracy returned to Chile, assets in the pension system shot up. Not only were reforms not canceled; they were intensified, adopted, and adapted.

Put another way, the great lesson to be learned from Chile is this extraordinary combination of pragmatism and continuity, the emergence of possibilism, a new style of conducting political economy. This is a combination that other countries, Mexico and Brazil especially, seek to share.

In Mexico, pragmatism shone through in the mid 1990s with the signing of a free-trade agreement with the United States and Canada. For the first time in history, a country from the South signed a free-trade accord with two countries from the North. Latching on to an economic powerhouse and the world's leading democracy was a major undertaking for Mexico, comparable to that experienced by Spain as the European Union allowed the economy to benefit from an anchor of external credibility. In 2000, Mexico underwent a change of government without an economic crisis—an event not heard of before in a country where the cycle of political change every 6 years had been accompanied by financial turbulence. Throughout the 1990s and the early 2000s, Mexico also achieved what no other country in the region had managed to do until then: break the spell cast by the political cycle.

Likewise, in Brazil recent governments carried out important pragmatic adjustments. The most spectacular of these was the one carried out by Lula's government. In 2002 the financial markets feared Lula's rise to power, but his monetary orthodoxy and his fiscal policy surprised everyone. In 2004, Brazil's economy grew at a rate of about 5 percent. The reforming impulse was very strong, and several important fiscal, pension, and banking reforms managed to overcome the parliament's "test of fire." Lula's social programs and his investment in infrastructure, although criticized, were in line with the promises made by the government for more just, more efficient, better distributed growth. Beyond the political noise in Brazil, what draws one's attention in recent years is the combination of fiscal and monetary orthodoxy with social policies. This combination drew attention not only from the financial markets and foreign investors but also from Latin American politicians, particularly those on the left. In Uruguay, a left-wing government claiming to be pragmatic in this way came into power. It is an open question if Lula will be reelected again in 2006. Whoever wins the presidency, the pragmatic and gradual course

will not change. The anchoring of the political economy
of the possible in Brazil could be contagious throughout
Latin America, resulting in the spread of pragmatic, continuing, and gradualist economic policies. In a region
that has been made dizzy by frequent changes in ideological paths, this would be great news.

Chile, Brazil, and Mexico now have powerful compasses to help them keep their bearings and sail away
from the rocky coastlines where the populist sirens sing.
This trio could be inspirational to other Latin American
countries. In 2006, as most Latin American countries elect
new leaders, the stars of the possible should continue to
shine on firmly and brightly in the Latin American sky.

An Unfinished Journey

The emergence of possibilism, however, remains incomplete and fragile; it is an unfinished journey. It is also part
of a more profound shift, as consequential as the fall of
the Berlin Wall. It entails a fin-de-siècle skepticism with
promises, at the end of a century marked by the ebb of
messianic attitudes and of great teleological projects. The
most notable observation that we can make on Latin
America is its genius for experimenting with the entire
range of possible hybridization between foxes and
hedgehogs. The neo-populist pragmatic chameleon is
really no more than the surprising and incongruous
grafting of Latin American possibilism at the end of the

twentieth century and the beginning of the current one. Unlike previous populist leaders, the neo-populists have been dealing in a much more pragmatic way with the constraints of the globalized world, conscious that that they cannot anymore overplay short-term promises and gains without inflicting medium-term disillusion and pain. (And citizens are no longer lured by intertemporal promises of all gain and no pain.) Of course one could object that such a graft is impossible, and that never in human history have we seen a hedgehog bred with a fox resulting in the birth of a chameleon. Nevertheless, life, everyday life, in small things as well as important ones, always exceeds our imagination.

When the wind blows, sometimes the foundations of our beautiful theories and our grand conceptualizations fall down like sand castles. Then we may complain of not having been able to keep this flood of water behind lock and key, about not trapping it in the nets of our paradigms. We may also be glad about some things: for instance, about the exposure of the lies inflicted by history on our macroeconomic textbooks, where we can read that the loving encounter between populism and neo-liberalism is theoretically impossible. Nevertheless, in the actual contemporary economic and political life of Latin America, these encounters have taken place. Even better, these encounters have given birth to a surprisingly strange chameleon whose colors do not cease to defy the laws of economic gravity and display all the shades of real life.

Above all, Latin America appears to be accomplishing a substantial if silent transformation. In the lost decade of the 1980s, and in the roaring 1990s, some countries in the region experienced a conversion to possibilism. Sometimes in a voluntary and deliberate way, other times without knowing it or even desiring it, political economy has become eminently pragmatic.

Chile exemplifies better than any other Latin American country this great, ongoing transformation. As noted earlier, this country has experienced a deluge of paradigms, from "revolution in liberty" to "socialist revolution," until coming across, already weary, the "neoliberal revolution." Nevertheless, beginning in the 1980s and especially over the course of the 1990s, its economic policies became more pragmatic and the country accumulated heterodoxies. Chile, like other countries in the region, did not simply move from the paradigm of the Good Revolutionary to that of the Good Free-Marketeer: it entered a crisis in the 1980s, a dead end that exemplified precisely the political economy of the impossible, the same idea that other countries have grappled with of implementing economic policies based on intangible macroeconomic paradigms and key slogans transformed into prêt-à-penser, ready-made, and quick fixes.

Throughout Latin America, the discourses of disenchantment with the promises of tomorrow have multiplied. The Mexican novelist Carlos Fuentes, among many others, has unequivocally decreed the defeat of utopian mechanics in the region: "Hegelians by day and epicureans by night, the governments of our economic booms believed that the path of history toward perfection and progress would bring us, in equal parts, liberty, well-being, and happiness; the miracles forged by the capitalist, Marxist or mixed-economy magicians were yet more mirages."[2] There are numerous examples of this newly minted conversion inhabiting the region, as Hirschman points out in an essay devoted to the evolution of development economics in Latin America, illustrating his argument with examples from Argentina, Brazil, and Chile.

If Hirschman's work rekindles interest, it is precisely because there has been a profound change unleashed in Latin America in the last two decades. With the ideological disarmament that culminated with the fall of the Berlin Wall in 1989, a certain style of political economy came under scrutiny. Beginning with his concrete observations in Brazil, Colombia, and Chile at the end of the 1950s, Hirschman characterized this style as rupturist, based essentially on the idea that reality can be perfectly perceived only through the prism of paradigms; a non-gradual economic style in which reiterated attempts and failures create a propensity for pessimism and defeatism (fracasomanía) through escalating ideologies. Attempts to accelerate the rate of development through "pseudocreative answers," definitive and quick integrated solutions, put aside the possible cumulative consequences and the possible lessons derived from previous experiences.

Yesterday the pragmatist collages of Mexican leaders, and today the serene face of Lagos in Chile or the radiant one of Lula in Brazil, all appear to point to a possible path that combines laissez-faire policies with state intervention, neo-liberal recipes with social condiments. The range of these of the possible also appears to be relatively broad, as the diversity of the trajectories confirm. The Colombia of Alvaro Uribe is courageously and firmly dedicated to ending the endemic violence that drains the economic and democratic bases of the Andean country. Uruguay, under the government of Tabaré Vázquez and his finance minister Danilo Astori, for the first time in its history of nearly 200 years, inaugurated a leftist coalition in 2005, introducing orthodox policies in fiscal and monetary matters. These examples illustrate the insistent rejection of magical formulas and monolithic responses to resolving the problems and the challenges these countries face.

The magic key that opens the doors to the paradise of development has not been found. Perhaps this is because for many years an attempt was made to find a single key that would open all the doors and solve all the challenges at once. As Ricardo Hausmann, Dani Rodrik, and Andrés Velasco emphasize in their recent work, it is useless to attempt to identify and apply an infallible and unique growth strategy, a unique and magical formula applicable to all countries.

There have been similar attempts use the same recipes in all Latin American countries, savory or sweet and in the same proportion, depending on the culinary economic fashion of the moment, and on the atmosphere prevalent in a distant, Northern corner of the West. The same dishes have been served to all countries in the region, with a strong dash of ideology added as condiment. Even if one acknowledges that these dishes have sometimes been reheated successfully and astutely for the more tropical or Andean climates in Latin America, the beginning of this millennium attests to the indigestion that often follows these culinary feasts. Argentina is a vibrant example.

There is no development process that is unquestionably good: some are simply less bad than others, according to the local contexts. Nor is there a systematic correlation between political democracy and economic development, nor global trade laws that are valid everywhere. Perhaps it would be better to forget the idea of a succession of supposedly ideal sequences and to opt for reforms that are not only cumulative but also adaptive. The great lesson of Latin America in the last years was inherent to this emergence—albeit unfinished, diffuse, and incomplete—of a political economy of the possible. To paraphrase the great Peruvian novelist Mario Vargas Llosa, who once dreamed of directing his country's destiny, paradise is not around the next corner. Paradise is not of this world, even though we can perhaps see its reflection on a canvas by Hieronymus Bosch or in the smiles exchanged between lovers. El Dorado was not found and would never have been found, either in space or in time.

To insist upon its arrival by forcing reality and applying shock therapies—whether socialist or neo-liberal models (do-it-yourself kits, as Julio Cortázar would say)—to impose on reality, was, in the end, only another way of not to love life.

It is possible that, as Rodrik writes in arguing for reinventing industrial policies in the twenty-first century, we are on the eve of a historic opportunity. The firm convictions of the apostles of free trade and monetarist shock therapies have vanished, as have those of the talibans of interventionism and regulation. The adventurism of import-substitution strategies and of state planning and interventionism has reached its limits, leading to painful one-way streets and economic crises. Few serious economists believe today in public spending as the single engine for development. In the same way, liberalization and de-regulation at all costs is certainly beneficial to export activities and helps strengthen the financial sector, but it also produces fearful boomerang effects, as the International Monetary Fund recognizes, when these policies are not properly implemented. The new era therefore seems to demand more pragmatic solutions and also to require more imaginative realism.

One of the keys to economic development resides, without doubt, in institutional innovations. An avalanche of studies flows into developing countries today to explain how fundamental political and economic institutions are unraveling the mystery of development. Once the pendulum shifted from all State solutions toward all market-based solutions, the resurgence of institutions pointed to a more balanced position. No doubt it is beneficial to distrust these new systematic explanations and to question assumptions when these begin to take on the attributes of infallible laws, as Adam Przeworski points out. This healthy skepticism does not mean, however, that these explanations focused on institutional anchors are not fundamental frameworks for the understanding of economic and political development. A wide range of institutions were considered, such as those involved in the consolidation of property rights; the implementation of adequate processes and incentives, with the goal of holding decision-makers accountable; and the development of mechanisms to increase the quantity and quality of information relative to governmental actions to and thus allow for clear judgment on the part of the citizens.

The experiences of Chile, Mexico, Brazil, Uruguay, Colombia, Argentina, Venezuela, Bolivia, Peru, and Ecuador attest to the importance of this institutional ferment when evaluating policy successes and failures. These are precarious processes, formed gradually and in spite of setbacks, inscribed in different periods and historical destinies. It is essential to understand that institutions function as engines for reform, but also as inhibitors of populist drifts. Institutions can channel reforming impulses, but can also neutralize or inhibit short-term pulsations, helping to avoid the search for shortcuts in matters of political economy by combining technical and political rationality.

In tying its hands to the institutional masts, these two rationalities limit each other, and from this combination the possibility of viable development and pragmatic policy making processes emerges. This combination is decisive at the time of starting successful or failed reforms. Citing his own experiences, Brazil's Fernando Henrique Cardoso said that the success of the Real Plan was not only tied to monetary stabilization. In a subtler way, it was also linked to the implementation of processes that reinforced the deliberative capacity of institutions and increased the technical capacity of the legislative powers and the decision-making powers of the executive. One of the keys to development lies in the reinforcement of democratic government by strengthening and nourishing the interaction between technical and political rationalities.

It is a matter of achieving a subtle equilibrium that is not characteristic in developing countries but which is especially important to them. In countries where poverty and inequality predominate, political rationality tends to center on short-term dividends, especially when reforms generate new demands that are superimposed on the old ones. In this way, the presence of populist practices and rhetoric in the context of relatively weak institutions tends to inhibit technical rationality. The combination of these two rationalities is even more important if we remember that one can succumb to two equally nefarious temptations, either ignoring political rationality in favor of technical rationality alone or vice versa. In countries where the combination of these two types of rationality is balanced with formal and informal institutional mechanisms (Chile, Brazil, and Mexico, for example), the possibilist economic policies are deployed efficiently. In contrast, these policies are inhibited or altered when the combination loses its equilibrium in favor of one or the other rationality (a situation seen in Argentina and Venezuela during the 2000s). This disequilibrium is even more destabilizing when it takes place in contexts of low institutional density and cognitive weakness. The risks of falling down are intensified even more when, under the pressure of urgency and the proliferation of demands, technical and political rationality are overwhelmed by the search for populist expediency.

One of the enduring difficulties lies in the temporal variable. In many ways, the idea of time as political capital fails. Under the double pressure of the electorate and investors, Latin American leaders are committed to a dual race against the clock. They must gain and keep the confidence of the citizenry by showing quick results, particularly in the social arena. At the same time, they must gain the trust of the investors, domestic and foreign, who demand equally fast macroeconomic results—results that sometimes conflict with social goals. How can a country win two races held simultaneously on the same great stage of development when the social and economic clocks are set to different measures—or, even worse, when the clocks that gauge the race move in opposite directions?

The structural reforms that have taken place in the region have certainly adjusted Latin America's clocks to global time. Nevertheless, a great number of Latin Americans continue to lack the most elemental tools that would allow them to enjoy being synchronized with the schedules of global time. They lack the basics: education, sanitation, infrastructures, and income. The 1990s brought surprising structural advances and reforms of great scope. But the 1990s were also years of brutal financial crises, with growth rates that did not translate into identical terms for all sectors of the region's population. Ultimately, what was most surprising was people's tolerance for situations that did not improve, their remarkable endurance, and the political economy of patience at which they proved themselves adept at practicing.

It is likely that there resides here another illustration of the "tunnel effect" which I wish to address in my conclusion. Those who are in the tunnel of underdevelopment and have reason to believe it will come to an end because they have heard that some travelers have gone from tourist to business class, keep on waiting, and are willing to endure this adverse situation. As long as there are mechanisms of social mobility, the "tunnel effect" works and the tolerance for inequality can be surprisingly high. But the ability to endure can be eroded because the tunnel may prove to be endless and the social elevator may have broken down. The decline of democratic loyalties and the proliferation of anti-political protests are definitely proof of this erosion. For many, the silence of the

sirens can seem maddening, as shown by the success of
the calls to re-enchantment from Argentina to Venezuela
and from Bolivia to Ecuador, especially when these calls
are accompanied by the consciousness that it is not possible to trespass from tourist to first class. What is even
worse is the possibility that the light seen at the end of
the tunnel may not be daylight but the light of a train
traveling at full speed in the opposite direction.

It is possible that this tunnel effect is losing force in
Latin America. But it is also possible that this decline
may not lead to the disaster announced by some and that
the silence of the sirens of hopes, may not be quite so
maddening. But for this to take place, once again it will
be necessary to invent and to imagine trespassings and
auto-subversions and to continue to seek with curiosity
and humbly forget, like Ulysses, the majestic sirens'
song. With wile and calculation, in spite of the shoals, we
know that Ulysses, a metaphorical figure of the political,
finally arrived at his destination. It is possible that the
modern version of the current trajectory of Latin
America's political odyssey was described by Kafka in
"The Silence of the Sirens," where the sirens no longer
sing and remain mute. To face this silence of contemporary politics, it will not be enough to plug one's ears with
wax and be tied to the masts. It will also be necessary to
keep a place in one's heart for a "bias for hope" and for a
"little more reverence for life," as Hirschman eloquently
and beautifully put it. In fact, the political economy of
the possible advocates for tempered optimism, bearing

in mind that the journey toward progress and development is long. Sometimes it is necessary to create an ad hoc solution with the means on board, without the help of the wind, going against the current. The most difficult task will be that of remaining open to the sirens' silence, not waiting in despair for the arrival of bright, shiny mornings.

In the basement of the Prado, Bosch's triptych hangs silently, while visitors gaze at it in wonder. Looking at it closely, one is astonished: the tree of the Americas hides a jungle, an infinite variety of countries, situations, and experiences. During this present decade not all of them will attain the peak of growth or the nirvana of prosperity, and not all will arrive to a safe haven. Nevertheless, some seem to have discarded a persistent illusion of social utopias and economic paradigms, the keys to the dreams (and the nightmares) that too often have only opened Pandora's box containing endless purgatories and painful economic hells. The paradise is not around the corner, but there may be a singular bias for hope for Latin America's immediate future.

Notes

Introduction

1. Rorty, *Philosophy and Social Hope*, p. 30.

Chapter 1

1. Berlin, "Crooked Timber," p. 1.

2. Rangel, *The Latin Americans*, p. 9.

3. Hirschman, *Journeys toward Progress*, pp. 240, 241.

Chapter 2

1. Tocqueville, *Democracy in America*, pp. 352–356.

2. Przeworski et al., *Democracy and Development*.

3. Hirschman, "The Changing Tolerance," p. 545.

4. Rigobón and Rodrik, "Rule of Law, Democracy, Openness, and Income."

Chapter 3

1. Berlin, *Crooked Timber*, p. 212

2. Gutiérrez was forced out of the presidency in April 2005.

Chapter 4

1. Góngora, Ensayo histórico, p. 270.

2. Díaz-Alejandro, "Some Unintended Consequences of Financial Laissez-Faire," p. 91.

3. In recent years he has been on the staff of the conservative-libertarian Cato Institute.

4. Constant, *Political Writings*, p. 157.

Chapter 6

1. Fuentes, *A New Time for Mexico*, p. 69

2. An emerging market bond spread is the difference in yield between US Treasury notes (maturing in 10 years) and Treasury notes of emerging markets (with the same maturity). The higher the spread, the greater the investment risk. By mid 2005, Chilean spreads, the lowest in Latin America, were around 50 basis points, while Brazilian ones were around 400 basis points. During the Brazilian crisis of 2002, the spread exceeded 2,000 basis points.

Chapter 7

1. Hirschman, *A Bias for Hope*, p. 29.

2. Hirschman, *A Propensity to Self-Subversion*, p. 183.

3. Ibid., p. 184.

4. Weber, *Politics as a Vocation*, p. 44.

Chapter 8

1. There are nearly 20,000 Cuban doctors in Venezuela.

Conclusion

1. Berlin, *Russian Thinkers*, p. 78.

2. Fuentes, *Valiente mundo nuevo*, pp. 16–17.

Bibliography

Acemoglu, Daron, Simon Johnson, and James Robinson. "Reversal of Fortune: Geography and Institutions in the Making of the Modern World Income Distribution." *Quarterly Journal of Economics* 117, no. 4, 2002: 1231–1294.

Acemoglu, Daron, Simon Johnson, James Robinson, and Yunyong Thaircharoen. "Institutional Causes, Macroeconomic Symptoms: Volatility, Crises and Growth." *Journal of Monetary Economics* 50, no. 1, 2003: 49–123.

Aggarwal, Vinod, Ralph Espach, and Joseph S. Tulchin, eds. *The Strategic Dynamics of Latin American Trade*. Stanford University Press, 2004.

Babb, Sarah. *Managing Mexico: Economists from Nationalism to Neoliberalism*. Princeton University Press, 2004.

Baily, Samuel L. *Immigrants in the Lands of Promise: Italians in Buenos Aires and New York City, 1870–1914*. Cornell University Press, 1999.

Barndt, William. Executive Assaults in South America: Modernization and Micro-Level Democratic Breakdown. Unpublished paper, Department of Politics, Princeton University, 2003.

Benhabib, Jess, and Adam Przeworski. "The Political Economy of Redistribution under Democracy." *Journal of Economic Theory*, forthcoming.

Berlin, Isaiah. *Four Essays on Liberty*. Oxford University Press, 1969.

Berlin, Isaiah. "The Hedgehog and the Fox." In Berlin, *Russian Thinkers*. Viking, 1978.

Berlin, Isaiah. "The Decline of Utopias in the West." In Berlin, *The Crooked Timber of Humanity*, ed. H. Hardy. Knopf, 1991.

Blanchard, Olivier. Fiscal Dominance and Inflation Targeting: Lessons from Brazil. Working paper 10389, National Bureau of Economic Research, 2004.

Blomberg, Brock, Jeffry Frieden, and Ernesto Stein. "Sustaining Fixed Rates: The Political Economy of Currency Pegs in Latin America." *Journal of Applied Economics* 8, no. 2, 2005: 203–225.

Boix, Carles. *Democracy and Redistribution*. Cambridge University Press, 2003.

Boix, Carles, and Susan Stokes. "Endogenous Democratization." *World Politics* 55, no. 4, 2003: 517–549.

Bordo, Michael D., and Barry Eichengreen. Crises Now and Then: What Lessons from the Last Era of Financial Globalization. Working paper 8716, National Bureau of Economic Research, 2002.

Bordo, Michael D., Jeffrey G. Williamson, and Alan M. Taylor. *Globalization in Historical Perspective*. University of Chicago Press, 2003.

Broz, Lauwrence. "Congressional Politics of International Financial Rescues." *American Journal of Political Science* 49, no. 3, 2005: 479–496.

Caballero, Ricardo. *Macroeconomic Volatility in Reformed Latin America: Diagnosis and Policy Proposals*. Inter-American Development Bank, 2001.

Calvo, Guillermo. "Explaining Sudden Stop, Growth Collapse and BOP Crisis: The Case of Distortionary Output Taxes." Presented at Third Annual IMF Research Conference, Washington, 2002. Published in *IMF Staff Papers* 50, special issue, 2003.

Calvo, Guillermo. Crises in Emerging Market Economies: A Global Perspective. Working paper 11305, National Bureau of Economic Research, 2005.

Calvo, Guillermo, and Carmen Reinhart. "Fear of Floating." *Quarterly Journal of Economics* 17, no. 2, 2002: 379–408.

Calvo, Guillermo, and Ernesto Talvi. Sudden Stop, Financial Factors and Economic Collapse in Latin America: Learning from Argentina and Chile. Working paper 11153, National Bureau of Economic Research, 2005.

Calvo, Guillermo, Alejandro Izquierdo, and Rudy Loo Kung. Relative Price Volatility under Sudden Stops: The Relevance of Balance Sheet Effects. Working paper 11492, National Bureau of Economic Research, 2005.

Calvo, Guillermo, Alejandro Izquierdo, and Luis-Fernando Mejía. On the Empirics of Sudden Stops: The Relevance of Balance-Sheet Effects. Working paper 10520, National Bureau of Economic Research, 2004.

Camp, Roderic. *Mexico's Mandarins: Crafting a Power Elite for the Twenty-First Century.* University of California Press, 2003.

Cardoso, Eliana, and Rudiger Dornbusch, "Brazilian Debt Crises: Past and Present," in *The International Debt Crisis in Historical Perspective*, ed. B. Eichengreen and P. Lindert. MIT Press, 1989.

Cardoso, Fernando Henrique, "Consideraciones sobre reforma del Estado y gobernanza democrática." Presented at Asamblea Anual de Gobernadores del Banco Interamericano de Desarrollo, Lima, 2004.

Castañeda, Jorge. *Utopia Unarmed: The Latin American Left after the Cold War.* Knopf, 1993.

Centeno, Miguel, and Joseph Nathan Cohen. Neoliberalism and Patterns of Economic Performance: 1980 to 2000. Working paper, Princeton University, 2005.

Chang, Roberto, and Andrés Velasco. "A Model of Financial Crises in Emerging Markets." *Quarterly Journal of Economics* 116, 2001: 489–517.

Chong, Alberto, and Florencio López de Silanes, eds. *Privatization in Latin America: Myths and Reality.* Stanford University Press, 2005.

Clark, Ximena, David Dollar, and Alejandro Micco. "Port Efficiency, Maritime Transport Costs and Bilateral Trade." *Journal of Development Economics* 75, no. 2, 2004: 417–450.

Collier, Simon, William F. Sater, and Alan Knight. *A History of Chile, 1808–2002*. Cambridge University Press, 2004.

Constant, Benjamin. *De l'esprit de conquête et de l'usurpation (1814)*. Flammarion, 1986. [*Political Writings*, ed. B. Fontana, Cambridge University Press, 1988]

De Gregorio, José, Sebastián Edwards, and Rodrigo Valdés. "Controls on Capital Inflows: Do They Work?" *Journal of Development Economics* 63, winter 2000: 59–83.

della Paolera, Gerardo, and Alan M. Taylor. *Straining at the Anchor: The Argentine Currency Board and the Search for Macroeconomic Stability, 1880–1935*. University of Chicago Press, 2001.

della Paolera, Gerardo, and Alan M. Taylor, eds. *A New Economic History of Argentina*. Cambridge University Press, 2003.

della Paolera, Gerardo, and Alan M. Taylor. "Gaucho Banking Redux." *Economía: Journal of the Latin American and Caribbean Economic Association* 3, no. 2, 2003: 1–42.

de Soto, Hernando. *The Other Path: The Invisible Revolution in the Third World*. Harper & Row, 1989.

Devlin, Robert, Antoni Estevaderodal, and Andrés Rodríguez. *The Emergence of China: Opportunities and Challenges for Latin America and the Caribbean*. Inter-American Development Bank, 2005.

Dezalay, Yves, and Bryant G. Garth. *The Internationalization of Palace Wars: Lawyers, Economists, and the Contest to Transform Latin American States*. University of Chicago Press, 2002.

Díaz-Alejandro, Carlos. "Some Unintended Consequences of Financial Laissez-Faire." In *Development, Democracy, and the Art of Trespassing: Essays in Honour of Albert O. Hirschman*, ed. A. Foxley et al.. University of Notre Dame Press, 1986.

Djankov, Simeon, Rafael La Porta, Florencio López de Silanes, and Andrei Schleifer. "The Regulation of Entry." *Quarterly Journal of Economics* 117, no. 1, 2002: 1–37.

Djankov, Simeon, Rafael La Porta, Florencio López de Silanes, and Andrei Schleifer. "Courts." *Quarterly Journal of Economics* 118, no. 2, 2003: 452–517.

Domínguez, Jorge, and Chappell Lawson, eds. *Mexico's Pivotal Democratic Elections: Candidates, Voters and the Presidential Campaign of 2000.* Stanford University Press, 2004.

Dornbusch, Rudiger, ed. *The Open Economy: Tools for Policymakers in Developing Countries.* Oxford University Press, 1998.

Dornbusch, Rudiger, and Sebastián Edwards, eds. *The Macroeconomics of Populism in Latin America.* University of Chicago Press, 1992.

Dornbusch, Rudiger, and Alejandro Werner. "Mexico: Stabilization, Reform and No Growth." *Brookings Papers on Economic Activity* 1994, no. 1: 243–315.

Edwards, Sebastián. *Crisis and Reform in Latin America: From Despair to Hope.* Oxford University Press, 1995.

Edwards, Sebastián. "Exchange Rate Policies in Latin America: Fads, Fashions, and Disappointments." Presented at "Una Nueva Agenda de Desarrollo Económico para América Latina," Cumbre Iberoamericana, Salamanca, 2005.

Edwards, Sebastián. Establishing Credibility: The Role of Foreign Advisors. Working paper 111429, National Bureau of Economic Research, 2005.

Eichengreen, Barry. *Capital Flows and Crises.* MIT Press, 2003.

Eichengreen, Barry, and Michael Bordo. "Crises Now and Then: What Lessons from the Last Era of Financial Globalization?" Presented at conference in honor of Charles Goodhart, Bank of England, 2001. A revised version appears in *Monetary History, Exchange Rates, and Financial Markets*, ed. P. Mizen. Edward Elgar, 2004.

Eichengreen, Barry, and Ricardo Hausmann. *Other People's Money: Debt Denomination and Financial Instability in Emerging Market Economies.* University of Chicago Press, 2005.

Easterly, William, Norbert Fiess, and Daniel Lederman. "NAFTA and Convergence in North America: High Expectations, Big Events, Little Time." *Economía: Journal of the Latin American and Caribbean Economic Association* 4, no. 1, 2003: 1–53.

Elster, Jon. *Ulysses and the Sirens: Studies in Rationality and Irrationality.* Cambridge University Press, 1984.

Estevadeordal, Antoni, Dani Rodrik, Alan M. Taylor, and Andrés Velasco, eds. *Integrating the Americas: FTAA and Beyond.* Harvard University Press, 2004.

Evans, Carolyn, and James Harrigan. "Distance, Time, and Specialization: Lean Retailing in General Equilibrium." *American Economic Review* 95, no. 1, 2005: 292–313.

Ffrench-Davis, Ricardo. *Reforming the Reforms in Latin America: Macroeconomics, Trade, Finance.* St. Martin's Press, 2000.

Ffrench-Davis, Ricardo. *Economic Reforms in Chile: From Dictatorship to Democracy.* University of Michigan Press, 2002.

Ffrench-Davis, Ricardo. *Reforming Latin America's Economies: After Market Fundamentalism.* Palgrave, 2005.

Fitzgerald, Valpy, and Rosemary Thorp, eds. *Economic Doctrines in Latin America: Origins, Embedding and Evolution.* Palgrave Macmillan, 2005.

Flandreau, Marc, ed. *Money Doctors: The experience of International Financial Advising, 1850–2000.* Routledge, 2003.

Forbes, Kristin. One Cost of the Chilean Capital Controls: Increased Financial Constraints for Smaller Trade Firms. Working paper 9777, National Bureau of Economic Research, 2003.

Fourcade-Gourinchas, Marion, and Sarah L. Babb. "The Rebirth of the Liberal Creed: Paths to Neoliberalism in Four Countries." *American Journal of Sociology* 108, 2002: 533–579.

Foxley, Alejandro, Michael S. McPherson, and Guillermo O'Donnell, eds. *Development, Democracy and the Art of Trespassing: Essays in Honour of Albert O. Hirschman.* University of Notre Dame Press, 1986.

Fraga, Arminio. "Latin America since the 1990s: Rising from the Sickbed?" *Journal of Economic Perspectives* 18, no. 2, 2004: 89–106.

Freyre, Gilberto. *Order and Progress: Brazil from Monarchy to Republic.* Random House, 2006.

Frieden, Jeffrey, and Ernesto Stein, eds. *The Currency Game: Exchange Rate Politics in Latin America.* Johns Hopkins University Press, 2001.

Fuentes, Carlos. *Valiente mundo nuevo: épica, utopia y mito en la novela hispanoamericana.* Colección Tierra Firme, Fondo de Cultura Económica, 1990.

Fuentes, Carlos. *A New Time for Mexico.* Farrar, Straus and Giroux, 1996.

Glaeser, Edward L., Rafael La Porta, Florencio Lopez de Silanes, and Andrei Shleifer. Do Institutions Cause Growth? Working paper 10568, National Bureau of Economic Research, 2004.

Goldfajn, Ilán, and Gino Olivares. "Full Dollarization: The Case of Panama." *Economia* 1, no. 2, 2001: 3–29.

Góngora, Mario. *Ensayo histórico sobre la noción de Estado en el siglo XIX y XX.* Editorial Universitaria, 1986.

González, José Antonio, Vittorio Corbo, Anne Krueger, and Aaron Tornell, eds. *Latin American Macroeconomic Reforms: The Second Stage.* University of Chicago Press, 2003.

Graham, Carol, and Sandip Sukhtankar. "Does Economic Crisis Reduce Support for Markets and Democracy in Latin America? Some Evidence from Surveys of Public Opinion and Well Being." *Journal of Latin American Studies* 36, May 2004: 349–377.

Haber, Stephen, ed. *How Latin America Fell Behind: Essays on the Economic Histories of Brazil and Mexico, 1800–1914.* Stanford University Press, 1997.

Haber, Stephen. Mexico's Experiments with Bank Privatization and Liberalization, 1991–2003. Working paper, Stanford University, 2004.

Haber, Stephen, and Aldo Musachio. Foreign Banks and the Mexican Economy, 1997–2004. Working paper, Stanford University, 2005.

Haber, Stephen, Douglass North, and Barry Weingast. Political Institutions and Financial Systems: Theory and History. Working paper, Stanford University, 2003.

Haber, Stephen, Armando Razo, and Noel Maurer. *The Politics of Property Rights: Political Instability, Credible Commitments, and Economic Growth in Mexico, 1876–1929*. Cambridge University Press, 2003.

Hagopian, Frances, and Scott Mainwaring. *The Third Wave of Democratization in Latin America: Advances and Setbacks*. Cambridge University Press, 2005.

Harrigan, James, and Anthony Venables. Timeliness, Trade and Agglomeration. Working paper 10404, National Bureau of Economic Research 2004.

Hausmann, Ricardo, Lant Pritchett, and Dani Rodrik. Growth Accelerations. Working paper 10566, National Bureau of Economic Research, 2004.

Hausmann, Ricardo, Dani Rodrik, and Andrés Velasco. Growth Diagnostics. Working paper, John F. Kennedy School of Government, Harvard University, 2005.

Hawking, Stephen. *A Brief History of Time*. Bantam, 1998.

Hermet, Guy. *Le populisme dans le monde. Une histoire sociologique, 19ème–20ème siècle*. Fayard, 2000.

Hermet, Guy, Soledad Loaeza, and Jean-François Prud'homme, eds. *Del populismo de los antiguos al populismo de los modernos*. Colegio de México, 2001.

Heymann, Daniel, and Axel Leijonhufvud. *High Inflation*. Clarendon, 1995.

Hirschman, Albert. "Problem Solving and Policy-Making: A Latin American Style?" In *Hirschman, Journeys toward Progress*. Twentieth Century Fund, 1963.

Hirschman, Albert. *Journeys toward Progress*. Twentieth Century Fund. 1963.

Hirschman, Albert. *Development Projects Observed*. Brookings Institution Press, 1967.

Hirschman, Albert. *Exit, Voice and Loyalty: Responses to Declines in Firms, Organizations and States*. Harvard University Press, 1970.

Hirschman, Albert. "The Search for Paradigms as a Hindrance to Understanding." *World Politics* 22, no. 3, 1970: 329–343.

Hirschman, Albert. *A Bias for Hope: Essays on Development and Latin America*. Yale University Press, 1971.

Hirschman, Albert. "The Changing Tolerance for Income Inequality in the Course of Economic Development." *Quarterly Journal of Economics* 87, November 1973: 544–565. Reprinted in Hirschman, *Essays In Trespassing*.

Hirschman, Albert. "La matriz social y política de la inflación: elaboración sobre la experiencia latinoamericana." *El Trimestre Económico*, no. 187, 1980: 679–709.

Hirschman, Albert. "An Alternative Explanation of Contemporary Harriedness." In *Hirschman, Essays In Trespassing*. Cambridge University Press, 1981.

Hirschman, Albert. "The Political Economy of Latin American Development: Seven Exercises in Retrospection." *Latin American Research Review*, no. 22, 1987: 7–36.

Hirschman, Albert. "The Case against One Thing at Time." *World Development*, no. 18, 1990: 1119–1122.

Hirschman, Albert. "Un sage et salutaire abandon. Les évènements de l'Est et des pays du Sud." *Esprit*, November 1990.

Hirschman, Albert. *A Propensity to Self-Subversion*. Harvard University Press, 1995.

Hobbes, Thomas. *Leviathan: Parts I and II*. Liberal Arts Press, 1958.

Hummels, David. Time as a Trade Barrier. Working paper, Krannert School of Management, Purdue University, 2001.

Iaryczower, Matías, Pablo Spiller, and Mariano Tommasi. "Judicial Decision Making in Unstable Environments: Argentina, 1938–1998." *American Journal of Political Sciences* 46, no. 4, 2002: 699–716.

Inglehart, Ronald, and Christian Welzel. *Modernization, Cultural Change and Democracy*. Cambridge University Press, 2005.

Jones, Mark P., Sebastián Saiegh, Pablo T. Spiller, and Mariano Tommasi. "Amateur Legislators–Professional Politicians: The Consequences of Party-Centered Electoral Rules in a Federal System." *American Journal of Political Science* 46, no. 3, 2002: 656–669.

Kaminsky, Graciela L., and Carmen M. Reinhart. "Financial Crises in Asia and Latin America: Then and Now." *American Economic Review* 88, no. 2, 1998: 444–448.

Kaminsky, Graciela L., and Carmen M. Reinhart. "Financial Markets in Times of Stress." *Journal of Development Economics* 69, no. 2, 2002: 451–470.

Karl, Terry Lynn. *The Paradox of Plenty: Oil Booms and Petro-States*. University of California Press, 1997.

Kern, Stephen. *The Culture of Time and Space, 1880–1918*. Harvard University Press, 1983.

Knight, Alan. *Mexico: The Nineteenth and Twentieth Century*. Cambridge University Press, 2005.

Koselleck, Reinhart. *The Future Past: On the Semantics of Historical Time*. Columbia University Press, 2004.

Krugman, Paul. "Dutch Tulips and Emerging Markets." *Foreign Affairs* 74, no. 4, 1995: 28–44.

Kuczinski, Pedro Pablo, and John Williamson, eds. *After the Washington Consensus: Restoring Growth and Reform in Latin America*. Institute for International Economics, 2003.

Larraín, Felipe, ed. *Capital Flows, Capital Controls and Currency Crises: Latin America in the 1990s*. University of Michigan Press, 2003.

Larraín, Guillermo. *Chile: fértil provincial*. Random House Mondadori, 2005.

Lechner, Norbert. *Las sombras del mañana. La dimensión subjetiva de la política.* LOM Ediciones, 2002.

Lederman, Daniel, William Maloney, and Luis Servén, eds. *Lessons from NAFTA for Latin America and the Caribbean.* World Bank and Stanford University Press, 2005.

Levy-Yeyati, Eduardo, and Federico Sturzenegger, eds. *Dollarization: Debates and Policy Alternatives.* MIT Press, 2003.

Levy-Yeyati, Eduardo, and Federico Sturzenegger. "To Float or to Fix: Evidence on the Impact of Exchange Rate Regimes on Growth." *American Economic Review* 93, no. 4, 2003: 1178–1189.

Linz, Juan. *The breakdown of Democratic Regimes: Crisis, Breakdown and Reequilibration.* Johns Hopkins University Press, 1978.

Linz, Juan. "Democracy's Time Constraints." *International Political Science Review* 19, no. 1, 1998: 19–37.

Lora, Eduardo. Structural Reforms in Latin America: What Has Been Reformed and How to Measure It. Working paper 466, Research Department, Inter-American Development Bank, 2001.

Lora, Eduardo, and Mauricio Oliveira. "What Makes Reforms Likely: Political Economy Determinants of Reforms in Latin America." *Journal of Applied Economics* 7, 2004: 99–135.

Lora, Eduardo, and Mauricio Oliveira. The Electoral Consequences of the Washington Consensus. Working paper, Research Department, Inter-American Development Bank, 2005.

Lora, Eduardo, and Ugo Panizza. "Examen des réformes structurelles." *Problèmes d'Amérique latine,* no. 48, 2003: 107–134.

Lora, Eduardo, Ugo Panizza, and Myriam Quipse-Agnoli. "Reform Fatigue: Symptoms, Reasons, Implications." *Economic Review Federal Reserve Bank of Atlanta,* second quarter 2004: 1–28.

Martínez Gallardo, Cecilia. "Ministerial Turnover and Bargaining over Policy: Evidence from Latin America." Presented at annual conference of American Political Science Association, Chicago, 2004.

McMillan, John, and Pablo Zoido. "How to Subvert Democracy: Montesinos in Peru." *Journal of Economic Perspectives* 18, no. 4, 2004: 69–92.

Monaldi, Francisco, Rosa Amelia González, Richard Obuchi, and Michael Penfold. "Political Institutions, Policymaking Processes, and Policy Outcomes in Venezuela." Presented at conference on Political Institutions, Policy-Making Processes, and Policy Outcomes in Latin America, Madrid, 2004.

Naím, Moisés. "Washington Consensus or Washington Confusion?" *Foreign Policy*, no. 118, 2000: 86–103.

Norris, Pippa, and Ronald Inglehart. "The True Clash of Civilizations." *Foreign Policy*, no. 135, 2003: 62–67.

Norris, Pippa, and Ronald Inglehart. *Sacred and Secular: Politics and Religion Worldwide.* Cambridge University Press, 2004.

North, Douglass C. *Institutions, Institutional Change and Economic Performance.* Cambridge University Press, 1990.

North, Douglass C. *Understanding the Process of Economic Change.* Princeton University Press, 2005.

Ocampo, José Antonio. "Latin America's Growth and Equity Frustrations during Structural Reforms." *Journal of Economic Perspectives* 18, no. 2, 2004: 67–88.

Ocampo, José Antonio. *Beyond Reforms.* World Bank, 2005.

Olson, Mancur. *Power and Prosperity: Outgrowing Communist and Capitalist Dictatorship.* Basic Books, 2000.

Organisation for Economic Cooperation and Development. *The OECD Economic Survey of Chile, 2003.*

Organisation for Economic Cooperation and Development. *OECD Economic Surveys: Brazil* (2005).

Payne, Mark J., Daniel G. Zovatto, Fernando Carrillo Flórez, and Andrés Allamand Zavala. La política importa: Democracia y desarrollo en América Latina. Inter-American Development Bank, 2003.

Paz, Octavio. *The Labyrinth of Solitude*. Grove, 1962.

Paz, Octavio. *Posdata*. Siglo XXI, 1977.

Paz, Octavio. "Critique of the Pyramid." In *The Labyrinth of Solitude*. Grove, 1985.

Paz, Octavio. *In Search of the Present: Nobel Lecture 1990*. Harvest/HBJ Original, 1990.

Paz, Octavio. *The Other Voice: Essays on Modern Poetry*. Harcourt Brace Jovanovich, 1991.

Pocock, J. G. A. *Politics, Language and Time: Essays in Political Thought and History*. Athenaeum, 1971.

Pocock, J. G. A. *The Machiavellian Moment*. Princeton University Press, 1975.

Popper, Karl. *Open Societies and Its Enemies*. Princeton University Press, 1971.

Przeworski, Adam. *Democracy and the Market. Political and Economic Reforms in Eastern Europe and Latin America*. Cambridge University Press, 1991.

Przeworski, Adam. Some Historical, Theoretical, and Methodological Issues in Identifying the Impact of Political Institutions. Working paper, Department of Politics, New York University, 2004.

Przeworski, Adam. "The Last Instance: Are Institutions the Primary Cause of Economic Development?" *European Journal of Sociology* 45, no. 2, 2004: 165–188.

Przeworski, Adam. Economic Development and Transitions to Democracy. Working paper, Department of Politics, New York University, 2004.

Przeworski, Adam, Susan C. Stokes, and Bernard Manin, eds. *Democracy, Accountability and Representation*. Cambridge University Press, 1999.

Przeworski, Adam, Michael E. Alvarez, José Antonio Cheibub, and Fernando Limongi. *Democracy and Development: Political Institutions and Well-Being in the World, 1950–1990*. Cambridge University Press, 2000.

Ramírez, Mari Carmen. *Inverted Utopias: Avant-Garde Art in Latin America*. Yale University Press, 2004.

Rangel, Carlos. *The Latin Americans: Their Love-Hate Relationship with the United States*. Transaction Books, 1987.

Reinhart, Carmen, and Kenneth Rogoff. "Serial Default and the 'Paradox' of Rich to Poor Capital Flows." *American Economic Review* 94, no. 2, 2004: 53–58.

Reinhart, Carmen, Kenneth Rogoff, and Miguel Savastano. "Debt Intolerance." *Brookings Papers on Economic Activity*, 2003, no. 1: 1–74.

Remmer, Karen. "Elections and Economics in Latin America." In *Post-Stabilization Politics in Latin America*, ed. R. Roett and C. Wise. Brookings Institution Press, 2003.

Rey, Hélène, and Philippe Martin. Globalization and Emerging Markets: With or Without Cash. Working paper 11550, National Bureau of Economic Research, 2005.

Rigobón, Roberto. "The Curse of Non-Investment Grade Countries." *Journal of Development Economics* 69, no. 2, 2002: 423–449.

Rigobón, Roberto, and Dani Rodrik. Rule of Law, Democracy, Openness, and Income: Estimating the Interrelationships. Working paper 10750, National Bureau of Economic Research, 2004.

Rodrik, Dani, ed. *In Search of Prosperity: Analytic Narratives on Economic Growth*. Princeton University Press, 2003.

Rodrik, Dani. Industrial Policy for the Twenty-First Century. Working paper, John F. Kennedy School of Government, Harvard University, 2004.

Rodrik, Dani (with Murat Iyigun). "On the Efficacy of Reforms: Policy Tinkering, Institutional Change, and Entrepreneurship." In *Institutions, Development, and Economic Growth*, ed. T. Eicher and C. Penalosa. MIT Press, 2006.

Roett, Riordan, ed. *The Mexican Peso Crisis: International Perspectives*. Lynne Rienner, 1996.

Rorty, Richard. *Philosophy and Social Hope*. Penguin, 1999.

Sachs, Jeffrey, Aaron Tornell, and Andrés Velasco. "The Mexican Peso Crisis: Sudden Death or Death Foretold." *Journal of International Economics* 41, no. 3–4, 1996: 265–283.

Santiso, Carlos. "The Contentious Washington Consensus: Reforming the Reforms in Emerging Markets." *Review of International Political Economy* 11, no. 4, 2004: 828–844.

Santiso, Javier. "De la condition historique des transitologues en Amérique latine et Europe Centrale et Orientale." *Revue Internationale de Politique Comparée* 3, no. 1, 1996: 41–69.

Santiso, Javier. "Théorie des choix rationnels et temporalités des transitions démocratiques." *L'Année Sociologique* 47, no. 2, 1997: 125–149.

Santiso, Javier. "The Fall into the Present: The Emergence of Limited Political Temporalities in Latin America." *Time and Society* 7, no. 1, 1998: 25–54.

Santiso, Javier. "Wall Street and the Mexican Crisis: A temporal Analysis of Emerging Markets." *International Political Science Review* 20, no. 1, 1999: 49–72.

Santiso, Javier. "The Art of Trespassing and Self-Subversion: Hirschman's View of Development." *ECLAC Review*, no. 70, 2000: 91–107.

Santiso, Javier. "Le passé des uns et le futur des autres: une analyse des démocratisations mexicaine et chilienne." In *Démocraties d'Ailleurs*, ed. C. Jaffrelot. Karthala, 2002.

Santiso, Javier. *The Political Economy of Emerging Markets: Actors, Institutions and Financial Crises in Latin America.* Palgrave, 2003.

Santiso, Javier, and Jorge Blázquez. "Mexico: Is It an Ex-Emerging Market?" *Journal of Latin American Studies* 36, no. 2, 2004: 297–318.

Santiso, Javier, and Juan Martínez. "Financial Markets and Politics: The Confidence Game in Latin American Emerging Economies." *International Political Science Review* 24, no. 3, 2003: 363–395.

Santiso, Javier, and Schedler, Andreas. "Democracy and Time: An Invitation." *International Political Science Review* 19, no. 1, 1998: 5–14.

Santiso, Javier, and Schmitter, Philippe. "Three temporal dimensions to the consolidation of democracy." *International Political Science Review* 19, no. 1, 1998: 69–92.

Santiso, Javier, and Laurence Whitehead. Ulysses, the Sirens and the Art of Navigation: Political and Technical Rationality in Latin America. Working paper prepared for Inter-American Development Bank, 2005.

Santiso, Javier, Jorge Blázquez, and Javier Rodríguez. Angel or Devil? Chinese Trade Impact on Latin American Emerging Markets. Presented in 2005 at international confereces of World Bank, Banco de España, Inter-American Development Bank, and Latin American and Caribbean Economic Association.

Smith, Peter. *Democracy in Latin America: Political Change in Comparative Perspective*. Oxford University Press, 2005.

Spiller, Pablo, and Tommasi, Mariano. *The Institutional Foundations of Public Policy: An Intertemporal Approach with Application to Argentina*. Cambridge University Press, 2005.

Stein, Ernesto, and Jorge Streb. "Elections and the Timing of Devaluations." *Journal of International Economics*, May 2004: 119–145.

Stiglitz, Joseph. "Whither Reform? Towards a New Agenda for Latin America." *Revista de la CEPAL* 80, August 2003: 7–40.

Stokes, Susan Carol. *Mandates and Democracy: Neoliberalism by Surprise in Latin America*. Cambridge University Press, 2001.

Sturzenegger, Federico, and Mariano Tommasi, eds. *The Political Economy of Reform*. MIT Press, 1998.

Thorp, Rosemary. *Progress, Poverty and Exclusion: An Economic History of Latin America in the 20th Century*. Inter-American Development Bank, 1998.

Tocqueville, Alexis de. *Democracy in America*. Library of America edition, 2004.

Tornell, Aaron, Frank Westermann, and Lorenza Martínez Trigueros. NAFTA and Mexico's Economic Performance. Working paper 1155, CESifo, 2004.

World Bank. *Doing Business in 2003*. World Bank and Oxford University Press, 2003.

World Bank. *World Development Report 2004*. World Bank and Oxford University Press, 2004.

World Bank. *Doing Business in 2005*. World Bank and Oxford University Press, 2005.

Valdés, Juan Gabriel. *Pinochet's Economists: The Chicago School of Economics in Chile*. Cambridge University Press, 1995.

Valdés-Prieto, Salvador, ed. *The Economics of Pensions: Principles, Policies and International Experience*. Cambridge University Press, 1997.

Valdés-Prieto, Salvador, and Marcelo Soto. "The Effectiveness of Capital Controls: Theory and Evidence from Chile." *Empirica* 25, no. 2, 1998: 133–164.

Vial, Joaquín. Some Ideas about a New Policy Consensus in Latin America. Working paper, 2003.

Weber, Max. *Politics as a Vocation*. Fortress Press, 1965.

Weber, Max. *The Vocation Lectures: Science as a Vocation, Politics as a Vocation*. Hackett, 2004.

Weyland, Kurt, ed. *Learning from Foreign Models in Latin American Policy Reform*. Johns Hopkins University Press, 2004.

Whitehead, Laurence. *Characterizing Latin America*. Palgrave, 2006.

Williamson, John, and Pedro-Pablo Kuczynski, eds. *After the Washington Consensus: Restarting Growth and Reform in Latin America*. Institute for International Economics, 2003.

Yashar, Deborah. *Contesting Citizenship In Latin America*. Cambridge University Press, 2005.

Yermo, Juan, Indermit S. Gill, and Truman Packard, eds. *Keeping the Promise of Social Security in Latin America*. Stanford University Press and World Bank, 2005.

Index